LYRIC

The term 'lyric' has evolved, been revised, redefined and contested over the centuries. In this fascinating introduction, Scott Brewster:

- traces the history of the term from its classical origins through the early modern, Romantic and Victorian periods and up to the twenty-first century
- demonstrates the influence of lyric on poetic practice, literature, music and other popular cultural forms
- uses three aspects – the lyric 'self', love and desire and the relationship between lyric, poetry and performance – as focal points for further discussion
- not only charts the history of lyric theory and practice but re-examines assumptions about the lyric form in the context of recent theoretical accounts of poetic discourse.

Offering clarity and structure to this often intense and emotive field, *Lyric* offers essential insight for students of literature, performance, music and cultural studies.

Scott Brewster is Director of English at University of Salford. He has published widely on modern poetry, Irish writing, Gothic and psychoanalysis. His co-edited essay collection, *Irish Literature Since 1990*, is forthcoming.

THE NEW CRITICAL IDIOM

SERIES EDITOR: JOHN DRAKAKIS, UNIVERSITY OF STIRLING

The New Critical Idiom is an invaluable series of introductory guides to today's critical terminology. Each book:

- provides a handy, explanatory guide to the use (and abuse) of the term
- offers an original and distinctive overview by a leading literary and cultural critic
- relates the term to the larger field of cultural representation.

With a strong emphasis on clarity, lively debate and the widest possible breadth of examples, *The New Critical Idiom* is an indispensable approach to key topics in literary studies.

Also available in this series:

LYRIC

Scott Brewster

Routledge
Taylor & Francis Group

LONDON AND NEW YORK

In memory of Jean Armitt,
1928–2008

First edition published 2009
by Routledge
2 Park Square, Milton Park, Abingdon, Oxon OX14 4RN

Simultaneously published in the USA and Canada
by Routledge
270 Madison Ave, New York, NY 10016

Routledge is an imprint of the Taylor & Francis Group, an informa business

© 2009 Scott Brewster

Typeset in Series Design Selected by
Taylor & Francis Books
Printed and bound in Great Britain by
TJ International, Padstow, Cornwall

British Library Cataloguing in Publication Data
A catalogue record for this book is available from the British Library

Library of Congress Cataloging in Publication Data
Brewster, Scott.
Lyric / Scott Brewster. – 1st ed.
 p. cm. – (The new critical idiom)
Includes bibliographical references and index.
 1. Lyric poetry – History and criticism. 2. Lyric poetry – Themes, motives. 3.
Songs – Texts – History and criticism. I. Title.
   PN1356.B74 2009
   809.1'04 – dc22
          2008048534

ISBN 10: 0-415-31955-2 (hbk)
ISBN 10: 0-415-31956-0 (pbk)
ISBN 10: 0-203-62505-6 (ebk)

ISBN 13: 978-0-415-31955-3 (hbk)
ISBN 13: 978-0-415-31956-0 (pbk)
ISBN 13: 978-0-203-62505-7 (ebk)

CONTENTS

SERIES EDITOR'S PREFACE

The New Critical Idiom is a series of introductory books which seeks to extend the lexicon of literary terms, in order to address the radical changes which have taken place in the study of literature during the last decades of the twentieth century. The aim is to provide clear, well-illustrated accounts of the full range of terminology currently in use, and to evolve histories of its changing usage.

The current state of the discipline of literary studies is one where there is considerable debate concerning basic questions of terminology. This involves, among other things, the boundaries which distinguish the literary from the non-literary; the position of literature within the larger sphere of culture; the relationship between literatures of different cultures; and questions concerning the relation of literary to other cultural forms within the context of interdisciplinary studies.

It is clear that the field of literary criticism and theory is a dynamic and heterogeneous one. The present need is for individual volumes on terms which combine clarity of exposition with an adventurousness of perspective and a breadth of application. Each volume will contain as part of its apparatus some indication of the direction in which the definition of particular terms is likely to move, as well as expanding the disciplinary boundaries within which some of these terms have been traditionally contained. This will involve some re-situation of terms within the larger field of cultural representation, and will introduce examples from the area of film and the modern media in addition to examples from a variety of literary texts.

ACKNOWLEDGEMENTS

I would like to express my thanks to John Drakakis for his enthusiasm and wise counsel, and to Polly Dodson and Emma Nugent for their help and patience during the writing of this book. Colleagues at the University of Salford and the University of Central Lancashire have been very supportive, and I am also grateful to Tom Corns for his expertise on Caroline court culture. I owe a particular debt of gratitude to a number of people: to my parents, James and Susan, for their unwavering encouragement; to Bethany and Rowan, for their lyric interludes; and especially to Lucie Armitt, for all of the above, and more.

1

INTRODUCTION

Nowadays, if we use the term 'lyric' we usually mean the words of a song. Most dictionary definitions describe lyric in two ways: as denoting a short poem expressing the poet's own thoughts and feelings, or a composition that is meant to be sung. The notion of the lyric poet or the singer–songwriter sharing her or his deepest, most private sentiments has become predominant in modern culture. There are certain consistent features in definitions of lyric: it is characterised by brevity, deploys a first-person speaker or persona, involves performance, and is an outlet for personal emotion. Yet these definitions highlight a series of unresolved questions that have shaped the theory, practice and interpretation of lyric for many centuries. Is lyric about display and public entertainment; is it something that can be shared or is it a matter of private experience; is it something for others, or just for oneself?

The first definition stresses the subjective nature of the lyric form, in that it is a concentrated expression of individual emotion, while the second stresses its intersubjective character through its relation to music and public performance. The first meaning reflects a theory that developed in the later eighteenth century, which defined lyric in terms of heightened emotion and authentic sentiment, and presented it as a (usually brief) moment of intensified awareness. M. H. Abrams summarises this view: 'lyric is any fairly short poem, consisting of the utterance by a single speaker, who expresses a state of mind or a process of perception, thought, and feeling' (Abrams 1993: 108–9). This speaker can muse in solitude or, as in dramatic lyric, address another presence in a particular situation. As we shall see, however, the lyric persona is not to be confused with the poet her- or himself: the emphasis on the author's sincerity and authenticity has been profoundly questioned by literary and critical theory in recent decades. (This demystification of the figure of the autonomous artist owes a debt to earlier conceptions of lyric, as subsequent chapters demonstrate.) Whether the 'I' speaks alone or to others, expresses emotion directly or adopts an elaborate disguise, lyric is fundamentally concerned with the conditions and nature of address.

The connection with music acknowledges the etymological origins of lyric: the term derives from the Greek *lurikos* ('for the lyre'), where verses would be sung or recited to the accompaniment of a lyre. In its earliest form, then, lyric involved some form of appeal or address to others. This implies a very different aesthetic experience from that associated with the isolated individual, who speaks or sings alone. Although the link between poetry and music has gradually diminished since the Renaissance, the relationship between words and performance has remained central to the understanding of lyric. In keeping with its origins, this book sees lyric *as a performance*, and will pay close attention to the voices and structures of address that are heard or invoked in lyric texts.

LYRIC AND GENRE

Lyric has proved a problematic case for genre theory. At times it is treated as a timeless, universal aesthetic disposition, at others it is identified as a generic category clearly defined by its subject matter, formal features and purposes. Andrew Welsh proposes that '[l]yric is finally less a particular genre of poetry than a distinctive way of organizing language' (Welsh 1978: 21). Ancient

Greece classified lyric in various ways: Sappho's poems were arranged on the basis of their metre, while Pindar's lyrics were categorised according to the content, function and occasion of the poem (Harvey 1955: 159). The Roman rhetorician Quintilian catalogued lyric as one of eight poetic genres, but made no attempt to define its nature. In perhaps the best known classification, Aristotle divides literary genres into the epic, dramatic and lyric, even if he barely refers to the lyric in his *Poetics*. Lyric poetry is merely a minor component of tragedy, alongside plot, character, diction, reasoning and spectacle (Aristotle 1996: 11). Aristotle's silence makes lyric 'the problematic term in this triad' (Frow 2006: 59), since it remains unclear whether lyric is a mode of presentation of speech or an essential, 'natural' form. In the sixteenth century, Antonio Sebastiano Minturno located the lyric or 'melic' as one of three 'presentational modes' alongside the epic and the dramatic (Fowler 1982: 218), but later theorists imply that lyric is as much a state of mind as a poetic style. For Hegel, lyric discloses the inner world of an individual who is separated from a wider community, while for Viëtor lyric is a 'basic attitude' that expresses feeling (Hernandi 1972: 12). As Gérard Genette points out, Aristotle's tripartite division conflates *mode*, a linguistic category that describes the means of enunciation, with *genre*, a literary category that refers to formal and thematic features (Genette 1992: 60–72). Many modern theories of genre are founded on this conflation or confusion of categories, and neither of these systems of classification assigns lyric a proper place (Duff 2000: 3).

Modern theory has tended to distribute genres on the basis of divisions between lyric, dramatic and narrative (Fowler 1982: 236), and in recent decades there have been various attempts at the generic classification of lyric. Paul Hernandi's 'Map of Modes' represents lyric diagrammatically: a vertical axis connects 'meditative poetry' and 'quasi-dramatic monologue', while the horizontal axis lists 'songlike poems' and the 'objective correlative' (Hernandi 1972: 166). While lyric is positioned at the 'private' point of the 'Compass of Perspectives', its coordinates are determined in relation to the 'authorial' and 'interpersonal' bearings of the compass, which positions it at the uncertain boundary between the public and the private. Other critical accounts have deemed it impossible to provide a comprehensive generic account of the lyric form; Preminger and Brogan argue that the term should be understood as embracing a wide range of subgenres of poetic practice (Preminger and Brogan 1993: 713–27). René Wellek is more trenchant: 'One must abandon attempts to define the general nature of the lyric and the lyrical. Nothing beyond generalities of the tritest kind can result from it' (Wellek 1970: 225). Philip Hobsbaum concludes that, due to the wide range of verse patterns (including stanzaic forms and line lengths) used for modes of lyric verse from the Renaissance onwards, lyric 'cannot be of much use as a defining term, at least so far as metre is concerned' (Hobsbaum 1996: 178–79).

Yet this terminological looseness has constituted lyric's strength, and has underpinned its constant reinvention. Lyric practice has exploited its proximity to other genres, such as elegy, epigram or dramatic monologue, either through their similar forms or shared function and subject matter. Love, death and nature have remained staple features of lyric poetry. Equally, it has blurred the boundaries between 'serious' and 'minor', religious and secular lyric forms, which have borrowed freely from each other at various historical moments. Lyric can be viewed as an umbrella term under which a variety of verse forms shelter, and its flexibility has aided its gradual ascent through the generic hierarchy to become the dominant mode of modern poetry.

From the early nineteenth century onwards, lyric came to be identified as the very essence of poetry, the most intense, passionate and authentic poetic mode. In 'The Two Kinds of Poetry' (1833), John Stuart Mill sees lyric as the primordial, pre-eminent poetic form, exemplifying the maxim *Nascitur Poeta* ('a poet is born not made'):

> Lyric poetry, as it was the earliest kind, is also, if the view we are now taking of poetry be correct, more eminently and peculiarly poetry than any other: it is the poetry most natural to a really poetic temperament, and least capable of being successfully imitated by one not so endowed by nature.
>
> (Mill 1989: 57)

In 'What is Poetry?' (1833), Mill portrays narrative and rhetoric as inimical to lyric: ballads, which derive their interest from storytelling, are 'the lowest and most elementary kind of poetry', a poetry that appeals to 'childhood' and the 'childhood of society' (Mill 1973: 77). Those whose minds and hearts have the 'greatest depth and elevation' appreciate that, in contrast to the true picture of life conveyed by fiction, the 'truth of poetry is to paint the human soul truly' (*ibid.*: 78). In 1918, Charles Whitmore concludes that when the 'vitality' of lyric is extinguished, 'true poetry is practically at an end' and thus 'an examination of the lyric, and a definition of its peculiar qualities, would be likely to throw light on the nature of poetry itself' (Whitmore 1918: 584). Whitmore defines lyric as poetry at its most spontaneous, elevated and intense: 'in the pure lyric the imagination is wholly unhampered, wholly unalloyed ... the lyric is the union of concision and amplitude in a highly developed and recurrent metrical form' (*ibid.*: 595). This view contrasts sharply with Helen Gardner's valuation several decades later: she treats lyric as a minor literary form, and contends that a major poet cannot claim the title 'on a handful of lyrics however exquisite' (Gardner 1949: 3).

The panegyrics of Mill and Whitmore identify the features most commonly associated with lyric: it involves a first-person speaker, reveals personal feeling that is often articulated in the present tense, and is characterised by its brevity. Helen Vendler has recently elaborated on these lyric 'virtues': 'extreme compression, the appearance of spontaneity, an intense and expressive rhythm, a binding of sense by sound, a structure which enacts the experience represented, an abstraction from the heterogeneity of life' (quoted by Cook 2004: 579). This book demonstrates that these virtues are far from incontrovertible, however. Hegel declares in *The Philosophy of History* (1837, 1858) that lyric poetry is 'the expression of subjectivity' (Bergstrom 2002: 12), but the nature of that 'expression' has remained subject to debate. For many, lyric 'is the most autobiographical of all poetry ... undividedly the expression of the elemental emotions' (Schelling 1913: 245), but the lyric self has also been regarded as an elaborate construction rather than a product of sincerity and spontaneity. Catherine Ing's characterisation of the Elizabethan lyric

highlights the distinctions between these versions of poetic subjectivity. In the 'personal' lyric, 'the reader expects to find a
revelation of strong personal emotion, usually of an intimate
kind'. It is often longer than song lyric, and deals with 'subtleties
and intimacies of emotion requiring careful and often prolonged
expression'. It conveys a 'singular' occasion, and the reader senses
that 'we are sharing in a private and probably unusual experience
with a particular person'. In 'impersonal' lyric, the emotion or
situation should be generalised, and nothing should connect the
feeling intimately with an individual whose 'privacy might seem
to be invaded by the overhearing of his utterance'. Ing concludes:
'Lyric of the first type is a voice from the invisible, lyric of the
second type the speech of a personality' (Ing 1951: 15). Accounts
of lyric subjectivity tend to occupy various points of this spectrum
between the invisible voice and personal speech, and Chapter 1
explores the question of the lyric voice in detail.

Most modern definitions of the lyric treat it as a short poem
concerned with an isolated or singular experience. Elder Olson
identifies an inextricable connection between its formal concentration
and its subject matter:

> The peculiar nature of lyric poetry is related, not to its verbal brevity,
> but to the brevity of the human behaviour which it depicts. Its verbal
> brevity, in general, is a consequence of the brevity of its action.
>
> (Olson 1964: 2)

Lyric is seen as a suspension or interlude, a unique intensification
of literary language distinct from everyday experience. Arnold
Stein argues that 'the moment of happiness is a lyric moment,
and there are no adequate symbols or translations which can stand
for that lyric parenthesis' (Stein 1962: 185). This 'moment' is
separated from a larger narrative. Coleridge remarks in *Biographia
Literaria* that '[a] poem of any length neither can be, or ought to
be, all poetry' (Wimsatt and Brooks 1970: 434), while Edgar
Allan Poe declares that '[w]hat we term long poem is, in fact,
merely a succession of brief poetical effects' (Poe 1984: 15). For
Poe, lyric intensity cannot be found in long poems (Wimsatt and
Brooks 1970: 589). T. S. Eliot, however, dismisses any necessary

relation between brevity and the expression of the poet's thoughts and feelings: 'How short does a poem have to be, to be called a lyric?' (Eliot 1990: 97). Alistair Fowler points out that Renaissance tragedy contains lyric and narrative sections that are subsidiary to the main action, while Virginia Woolf's *To The Lighthouse* provides a good example of the 'lyrical' novel in the twentieth century (Fowler 1982: 60, 211). As Chapter 4 demonstrates, Wordsworth's *Prelude* complicates distinctions between the self-contained lyric moment and narrative momentum in the long poem. Epic and longer narrative poems are now rare, but we still need to distinguish between short lyrics and extended lyric sequences, such as John Berryman's *The Dream Songs*, Douglas Dunn's *Elegies* or Tony Harrison's *School of Eloquence*. These qualifications suggest that brevity is not necessarily the signature of lyric.

Given these difficulties in classifying lyric as a genre or sub-genre, and in identifying its characteristics, the task of defining the term lyrical, possibly the 'most lawless category' (Rhys 1913: vi), becomes highly problematic. Novels, films, musical compositions, dance routines or visual art can all be designated lyrical by critics, usually meaning that these works seem impassioned, melodic, inspired, high-flown, enthusiastic, and so on. Yet if the term can be applied to a range of non-poetic art forms, its value in specifying the properties particular to lyric is called into question. As David Lindley acerbically comments: 'It is no doubt vain to hope for a ban on the modal use of "lyrical" outside very specific contexts, but it is hard to see what effort of discrimination could make it useful' (Lindley 1985: 24).

LYRIC AND HISTORY

The notion that lyric is the primordial essence of pure poetry is part of a wider tendency in the modern period to characterise lyric as capturing fundamental, enduring human emotions, and to assume that it is an unchanging aesthetic category. For example, W. R. Johnson declares it 'immutable and universal. Its accidents may and always do show extraordinary variations as it unfolds in time, but its substance abides' (Johnson 1982: 2). Yet assumptions about lyric are far from timeless. Lindley stresses the importance of historicising lyric practice: 'the only proper way to use the term "lyric" is with precise historical awareness ... As critics we can only attempt to be scrupulous in always using a generic term like "lyric" with the fullest possible historical awareness' (Lindley 1985: 84). Fowler points out that lyric, as defined by literary theory from Cicero to Dryden, must 'not be confused with the modern term' (Fowler 1982: 220), and our recent understanding of lyric is largely a product of the nineteenth century, when it became the 'dominant mode' of literature (*ibid.*: 206). The traditional privileging of lyric as 'immutable and universal' has led many critics to view lyric as a reactionary mode which seeks to 'exclude history and otherness' (Jeffreys 1995: 198).

Yet it is reductive to claim that lyric ignores or refuses the conflicts and discontinuities of history. Subsequent chapters demonstrate that in certain periods, competing ideas about lyric have coexisted, and conceptions and valuations of lyric have often shifted to accommodate changing historical conditions. Francis Turner Palgrave's *The Golden Treasury* of 1861 used the achievements of English lyric as a means of burnishing imperial power. Palgrave ends his Preface in expansive mode: 'wherever the Poets of England are honoured, wherever the dominant language of the world is spoken, it is hoped that they will find fit audience' (Palgrave 1964: xii). Palgrave homogenises the cultural difference that comprises 'English' literature, and also overlooks the multi-linguistic and transnational roots of English lyric. As we shall see, the earliest English lyrics are Anglo-Saxon laments influenced by Northern European poetic practice; medieval lyric was a blend of 'imported' and indigenous forms; while the modern lyric tradition originated in Provence and was refined in Italy and France before arriving on English shores. The long tradition of English love lyrics is the legacy of not only classical writers such as Sappho, Horace and Ovid, but also medieval writers such as Petrarch (1304–74) and Pierre de Ronsard (1524–85). Yet the rise and decline in the critical fortunes of lyric have often been linked to the expression of a sense of nationhood. For example, Ernest Rhys's *Lyric Poetry* and Frederick Schelling's *The English Lyric*, both published in 1913 at a time of acute international tension, consistently link the development of lyric to the national tale.

The fashioning of a 'national' lyric could also become entangled with gender politics: Margaret Dickie observes that in the United States, lyric tended to be treated as a minor, 'feminine' form, subordinate to the masculine epic in the attempt to articulate national ambition:

> Lyric poetry has been a neglected genre in American literary history. In the nineteenth century, it was regarded as insufficient to express the new country. The earliest call for an American literature in the 1830s and 1840s emphasized, above all else, length and the need for an impressive form to express a large country.
>
> (Dickie 1991: 7)

Similarly, in Victorian Britain, the isolated, private Romantic lyric came to be regarded as insufficiently masculine, socially engaged and productive at a time of imperial expansion (Byron 2003: 56). This perception echoed attitudes in the eighteenth century towards the 'effeminate' modern lyric's inferiority to the 'manly' epic, and this can be linked to Wordsworth's effort to 'remasculinise' the lyric in *Lyrical Ballads* (Patey 1993: 603–4).

Palgrave's *Treasury* is an attempt 'to include in it all the best original Lyrical pieces and Songs in our language, by writers not living – and none beside the best'. This canon-forming project claims to be 'acquainted with no strict and exhaustive definition of Lyrical Poetry', yet its definition of lyric has become the principal model in modern literary criticism: 'Lyrical has been here held essentially to imply that each Poem shall turn on some single thought, feeling or situation. In accordance with this, narrative, descriptive, and didactic poems – unless accompanied by rapidity of movement, brevity, and the colouring of human passion – have been excluded' (Palgrave 1964: ix). As Marjorie Perloff comments:

> The *Golden Treasury* can ... be seen as emblematic of the codification of Romantic theory, with its gradual privileging of the lyric above the other literary modes ... by the turn of the [twentieth] century, for most would-be practitioners of the craft in England and America, poetry meant Palgrave.
>
> (Perloff 1985: 177–78)

Yet this privileging of lyric is far from an inexorable development. Mark Jeffreys has commented that the most important transformations in the way that the term lyric was used took place in the early modern period: lyric emerges as a dominant category from a 'welter of shorter poetic genres', and it is only in the nineteenth century that it comes to be 'mythologized as the purest and oldest of poetic genres' (Jeffreys 1995: 197). Arthur Marotti observes that in Renaissance England, the lyrics produced by courtiers were treated as 'ephemeral "toys", usually not worth preserving' (Marotti 1991: 28). Lyric poems were written mainly for particular occasions, and hence were seen as having only momentary significance; it was only when these lyrics became 'enshrined in the fixity of print' that they could be termed 'literature' (*ibid.*: 36). Ironically, although Palgrave's definition affirms the Romantic theory of lyric, the Romantic period valued epic more than lyric, and Romantic women poets were until recently regarded as minor figures, partly because they eschewed the 'masculine' epic. The privileging of lyric in the nineteenth century was a response to the dominance of prose fiction, which superseded epic, the primary narrative poetic form: 'Lyric became the dominant form of poetry only as poetry's authority was reduced to the cramped margins of culture' (Jeffreys 1995: 200). The difficulty of providing a stable definition of lyric at different historical moments is also linked to changing critical tastes and assumptions. Jeffreys notes how the term lyric has disappeared from the title of poetic anthologies in recent decades, a situation that further complicates any attempt to identify a lyric canon: 'An abundance of texts can be found that fit the requirements of any definition of lyric, but no such definition satisfactorily includes all the well known poems considered lyric or lyrical' (*ibid.*: 203).

The inclination to subsume all poetic forms into the category of lyric is encouraged by anthologies that extract passages from long poems and present them as self-contained lyrics. This tendency led C. S. Lewis to lament readers' desire to regard *Paradise Lost* as a lyric, searching it for 'little ebullient patches of delight' (Matterson and Jones 2000: 83). The academy and the literary-critical industry have played a significant 'institutional' role in fostering the dominant version of the modern lyric. Tom Furniss and Michael Bath argue that increasingly we have been trained as readers to look for and value the personal, which privileges lyric over other genres. This understanding of lyric 'has served to reinforce the ideological distinction between the personal and the political' (Furniss and Bath 1996: 359). Additionally, Matterson and Jones observe that 'lyric, which can relatively easily be understood as a free-standing verbal object, is teachable in class in a way that, say, the epic or narrative poem is not' (Matterson and Jones 2000: 15). In its brevity and its stress on individual feeling, the lyric is also reflected in the majority of contemporary music we listen to. A correlation can thus be discerned between the presiding perception of lyric and our modern habits of learning and consumption.

This brief survey shows that, for such an apparently 'timeless' and 'universal' literary category, lyric is remarkably time-bound, and its generic classification cannot be dissociated from historical shifts in the use of the term. The variety of poetic forms examined in the book, ranging from ceremonial or occasion poems to brief, intense expressions of emotions and states of mind, illustrates the flexible way in which poets have adapted lyric. *Lyric* not only charts the history of lyric theory and practice, it also re-examines assumptions about the lyric form in the context of recent theoretical accounts of poetic discourse. The book offers a thematic and conceptual rather than strictly chronological account of lyric, although its structure clearly acknowledges distinct changes in understanding and practice. While it is possible to assert that there is 'no perceptible historical continuity' between, for example, troubadour and modernist lyrics (Jauss 1982: 108), certain recurrent issues surrounding lyric do arise at different historical moments: questions of voice and address, the nature of the poetic subject or persona, the role of lyric in its historical moment, its relation to performance, and its intersection with other forms of cultural representation. Thus the following chapters analyse lyric forms as performances, structures of address and complex interventions in the politics and philosophical debates of their historical moments.

Chapter 2 explores definitions and classifications of the term 'lyric' from its classical origins through to the late twentieth century. It shows how lyric involves a (rhetorical) performance and some relationship to another, as it is invariably an address to a lover, friend, absent or dead other, to an unspecified but implicit interlocutor – to some form of audience. Rather than restricting itself to generic categorisation, then, the discussion concentrates on defining lyric as an intense and highly self-conscious form of address. Since the Romantic period, the dominant understanding of lyric has postulated a speaker who is capable of conveying 'personal' thoughts and feelings in splendid isolation from other people, or from specific historical conditions. In contrast to this Romantic legacy, the chapter demonstrates that lyric is inter-subjective, since it is obliged to address itself to someone, and its represented or dramatised speaker/voice invariably is involved in a dialogue with an other. The present study unapologetically sustains the oral convention, or necessary fiction, of the speaking lyric 'I' by considering, for example, the soliloquy, the Victorian dramatic lyric, the modernist interior monologue, and the relation between lyric poetry and song.

Chapter 3 surveys a period in which generic classifications of lyric are shifting and unstable, and where it proves easier to dis-tinguish between different lyric genres than to advance a rigid and unified definition of lyric. It first discusses courtly poetry, which contains many of the central features associated with lyric, yet foregrounds artifice, irony, wit, detachment, skilful and inge-nious argumentation rather than immediacy or sincerity. The chapter also examines a more explicit version of lyric in perfor-mance, the dramatic soliloquy, which gives the moment of lyric intensity dramatic expression. It then shows how the metaphysi-cal lyric of Donne and others – in turns intimate, philosophically reflective and playful – is set against the various forms of ode developed in the later seventeenth and eighteenth centuries, which are often explicitly political or topical. Despite their dif-ferences, all these forms feature a speaker engaged in some act of eloquent persuasion or address, rather than in private meditation.

These opening chapters establish, and challenge, the pre-dominant late modern association of lyric with sincerity, intimacy and the direct expression of emotion and feeling. Chapter 4 demon-strates that, in practice, neither Romantic nor post-Romantic lyric poetry has renounced the rhetorical emphasis of early modern lyric forms. The modern lyric does not retreat 'inward': it continues to deploy modes of address that perform the self, from the apostrophe and dramatic monologue to the confessional poem. The poem of experience, whether the introspective short poem, the rapturous ode or the 'greater lyric', constitutes a conversation with or appeal to the other. The complex relationship between the self and the world is then traced in Victorian dramatic monologue and meditative verse, the defamiliarisation and impersonality of the modernist lyric, the 'staged' self in confessional poetry, and the fluid, ironic 'I' of innovative poetry in the contemporary period.

Chapter 5 develops the focus on the lyric self and its dialogue with the other by exploring the love lyric and poems which express intense emotions and passions that are amorous or spiritual, and which are driven by desire in both religious and secular forms. It traces the development of the courtly love tradition in English poetry through the conceit, the seduction poem and the aubade. The continuities and transformations of the love poem are examined from the initial reworking of the Petrarchan tradition in the sixteenth and seventeenth centuries through to the twenty-first century, including within contemporary popular music. The chapter also explores the tradition of devotional poetry, by examining lyrics that blend the secular and sacred, including hymns, elegies and meditations. The characteristic that connects these different forms of lyric desire is their shared yearning for transcendence, for the idealised object, for the inexpressible – a yearning nonetheless subject to both formal conventions and prevailing ideological assumptions about gender, sexuality, culture and power.

The final chapter considers lyric in performance. Ezra Pound declared that 'Poetry atrophies when it gets too far from music' (Pound 1961: 61). In spite of lyric's etymological connection with the lyre, the link between poetry and music has become mainly metaphorical for literary criticism, ever since the development of print fundamentally changed the relationship between music and poetry. The singing or recital of lyrics takes place in different contexts and produces different effects from those of the private reading experience, but the chapter shows that lyric has maintained a close relation to music and performance. It traces important residual features of the link between poetry and music from the medieval period to the present. Chapter 6 examines the public and performance aspects of lyric and considers lyric's relation to popular and dissident discourses. It stresses that some strands of contemporary poetry, such as song lyrics, performance and politicised poetry, correspond more closely to pre-Romantic conceptions of lyric than to dominant post-Romantic theories of the private lyric. This final chapter thus returns the discussion to its initial premise: it argues that lyric, far from presenting the unmediated thoughts and feelings of an isolated individual, centres on the relationship between the self and others, the self and history, and the self and language.

2

ORIGINS AND DEFINITIONS

We have seen how the theory and practice of lyric has not followed a continuous pattern of development, but it is possible to
trace a basic timeline for lyric from classical antiquity to the
present. The term 'lyric' emerges from Ancient Greece, where it
was theorised in Aristotle's *Poetics* (via an earlier Pindaric model of
lyric), then translated to Rome, through the poetry of Horace and
Catullus in particular. The subsequent development of lyric in
Europe assumed both religious and secular forms, where 'high' or
rarefied and popular or vernacular lyric forms often interacted.
The 'literary' lyric emerges in the music and poetry of the troubadours, and in the conventions of *amour courtois* (courtly love)
that moved from Italy and France to Britain in the early sixteenth
century, and produced a rich diversity of lyric and related forms.
The perceived decline of the lyric in the eighteenth century
merely preceded its apotheosis in the Romantic period, which has
shaped modern critical assumptions about the lyric mode. In this
major historical and philosophical moment, there is a profound
conceptual shift in the understanding of the lyric. As we shall see,
the dominant, post-Romantic understanding of lyric, with its
stress on interiority, feeling and solitude, minimises or effaces

those elements of performance, ceremonial or ritual associated with lyric prior to Romanticism, even if its modes of address, such as apostrophe, remain central to Romantic poetics. This chapter examines the interplay and tensions between dialogue and introspection, emotional sincerity and rhetorical display, and exposure and disguise that feature consistently in the theory and practice of lyric from its classical origins to the present.

THE ROOTS OF LYRIC

In ancient Greece, lyric was a specific generic term, referring to a 'song' sung to the accompaniment of a lyre. It was distinct from epic and drama, and from other poetic forms such as elegy, which was accompanied by the flute rather than the lyre (Lindley 1985: 5). The lyric mode could also be subdivided into solo songs, such as those identified with Sappho, or the choral songs of Pindar, although recent scholarship has suggested that Sappho's work, too, may have been performed with a chorus rather than by a single voice (Wilson 2004: 28). In Aristotle's *Poetics*, *melopoeia* (song) is the lyrical element of tragedy. In later lyric practice, the musical element of lyric became more vestigial. For example, the Roman poet Horace's songs (*carmina*) are not meant to be sung; while he reinvented Greek lyric, attempting to recreate its metres in Latin and translating its themes and conventions (Johnson 1982: 123), Horace is not lyrical in its strict earlier sense, not least because the Greek papyri to which he referred did not contain discernible musical notation. Even after poetry became primarily a matter of writing rather than oral performance, however, musicality continued to be regarded as a signature feature of the lyric. Writing in 1924, W. B. Sedgwick declared that Greek lyric exemplifies the qualities of true lyric poetry: 'simplicity and directness, a high rapture (the "lyric cry"), but above all, perfect harmony in diversity of metre, freedom of construction and apparent spontaneity, checked and held together by the binding force of musical rhythm.' With this gold standard in mind, all lyric poetry is 'inconceivable' without musical accompaniment (Sedgwick 1924: 97). Sedgwick's hymn of praise demonstrates the prevailing connection between words and music in definitions of lyric forms across almost three millennia.

Given the twin emphases on voice and performance, ancient lyrical forms often imply 'actual interpersonal relations' (Fowler 1982: 67). As George N. Shuster has pointed out, '[a]ll the verse of antiquity was addressed to somebody, primarily because it was either sung or read and the traditions of song and recitation required that there be a recipient' (Shuster 1940: 11–12). The identity of that speaking voice, and the nature of that address, have become recurrent questions in theories of lyric. W. R. Johnson observes that lyric in its earliest form discloses

> the conditions and the purposes of the song: the presence of the singer before his audience; his re-creation of universal emotions in a specific context; a compressed, stylised story ... and, finally, the sharing, the interchange of these emotions by singer and audience.
>
> (Johnson 1982: 4)

Ancient Greek poetry presents a 'situation of discourse' involving a speaker and a hearer, and resembles the situation of oratory. It is a matter of rhetorical performance rather than a naked expression of personality or an 'isolated *cri de coeur*' (*ibid*.: 30). This emphasis on lyric as discourse, involving description and deliberation rather than expression, is also linked to the *epideictic*, or display oratory, a poetry of praise, blame and evaluation. The epideictic orator, like the lyric poet, offers 'paradigms of identity', assuming a position or role from which to address an audience. Jeffrey Walker (1989) argues that Pindar's epideictic oratory, particularly in his victory odes, is the typical form of ancient Greek lyric, its rational persuasion elevated by music and patterned prosody, far from the rapturous 'cry' suggested by Sedgwick. For example, Horace uses the pronominal form and evokes the '*hic et nunc*' ('here and now') of Greek lyric and its tradition of music, performance and address (Johnson 1982: 127), in clear contrast to the retrospective 'emotion recollected in tranquillity' that characterises lyric for Wordsworth in his Preface to *Lyrical Ballads* (1798). Robert Langbaum stresses the dramatic quality of the classical lyric, and argues that it is not to be understood as purely objective; such 'objectivity' would make it indistinguishable from epic. In the work of Sappho, Pindar, Catullus or Horace, the poet–speaker 'talks, as in conversation, either about himself or about someone or something else; and he talks ... either to himself or to someone or something else' (Langbaum 1957: 46–47).

Greek lyric is thus not the poetry of 'pure' feeling or experience, since it depends upon a rhetorical performance and a structure of address; what mattered in Greek lyric 'was not the need to express something, but the desire, the choice, to conduct lyrical discourse' (Johnson 1982: 72). Yet in Aristotle's definition of the lyric in *Poetics*, which has become the dominant model for the modern period, the stress is placed on expression. For Aristotle, all poetry is a species of imitation, a staging of character in action. Lyric is a relatively minor component of tragedy and epic poetry, but its poetic quality lies in the capacity to reveal in exemplary fashion how a character behaves in a given situation. Walker terms the Aristotelian form of lyric a mini-drama, a scene or crucial moment 'abstracted from an implied enclosing story' (Walker 1989: 13), and it is this model that has become predominant in accounts of the scope and purpose of lyric practice. Lyric comes to describe a short poem that is neither narrative nor discursive, as in the epideictic mode. It is an utterance that is curiously 'outside' of time rather than tied to a specific occasion, an interlude in the main narrative, a self-expressive declaration directed towards an absent or imaginary presence rather than to a reader or listener. This paradigm of the non-discursive lyric has acquired critical supremacy, even if Pindar has been described by Harold Bloom as 'the truest paradigm for western lyric' (Bloom 1979: 17). In Walker's account, the privileging of interiority and introspection in Aristotle's rewriting of Pindaric lyric anticipates Romantic and post-Romantic conceptions of lyric, as we shall see in Chapter 4. However, later notions of lyric are shaped by both Pindaric and Aristotelian models. The contrasting ways of defining lyric in ancient Greece, as personal or public, temporally located or timeless, discursive or expressive, constantly resurface in later critical understandings of the term.

FROM SPEECH TO WRITING

The relationships, or tensions, between writing and music, 'public' and 'private' expression, sacred and secular purposes, and elite and popular forms have been central and recurrent features of the theory and practice of lyric from antiquity onwards. In its Christian phase, Rome bequeathed a number of types of lyric in the form of Latin homilies and hymns, but these operated alongside more vernacular traditions in North Africa and in southern and northern Europe. Peter Dronke (1968) has stressed the internationalism of religious and secular lyric practice between the ninth and fourteenth centuries in particular: strong and interconnected lyric traditions stretched from Iceland to Byzantium, Portugal to Russia and Ukraine, England to Italy, Spain to Poland, as well as to North Africa and the Middle East, often brought by poet–musicians travelling between courts and aristocratic households. As a consequence, lyric flourished in the Romance, Germanic, Arabic and Hebrew languages, and constituted a form of intercultural contact zone. While lyric could serve different sacred and secular purposes in each of these locations, the integral connection between words, music and performance remained a consistent feature of lyric practice. Religious lyrics were to an extent the preserve of the church and the conventionally learned, as most were written in Latin, but many were composed in vernacular tongues and coexisted with songs tied to secular festivals and seasonal celebrations.

In northern Europe, Germanic heroic verse was composed to be sung or spoken aloud as part of a public performance in a primarily oral culture. Its intersubjective point of view and narrative impetus mark it out as epic rather than lyric in form, but in a poem such as *Beowulf* there are recognisably lyric moments, typified by the elegaic intensity of the hero's funeral pyre:

> Black wood-smoke
> arose from the blaze, and the roaring of flames
> mingled with weeping. The winds lay still
> as the heat at the fire's heart consumed
> the house of bone. And in heavy mood
> they uttered their sorrow at the slaughter of their lord.
> (Alexander 1973: 150)

Another Anglo-Saxon poem, 'The Wanderer', is a dramatic monologue which conveys an individual's sense of isolation and displacement, resulting from the death of his lord; its opening and closing lines, which frame the monologue, imply a Christian perspective on the suffering described, but the main speaker recalls a pre-Christian heroic society. The poem grants an interiority and reflectiveness to its persona that is typical of later versions of lyric:

> Mindful of hardships, grievous slaughter,
> the ruin of kinsmen, the wanderer said:
> 'Time and again at the day's dawning
> I must mourn all my afflictions alone.
> There is no one still living to whom I dare open
> the doors of my heart.'
>
> (Crossley-Holland 1984: 50)

Another long poem, 'The Seafarer' (later translated by Ezra Pound), declares its Christian dedication more overtly, but like 'The Wanderer' its didactic quality is particularised by the intense sensory detail of icy seas and the harshness of the elements endured by the singer–speaker. The speaker sets out on his metaphorical journey of faith to 'sing a true song about myself' (*ibid*.: 53), suggesting a degree of self-consciousness that underlies the poem's functional purpose and formulaic pattern.

Many lyric and related forms are utilised in the Anglo-Saxon period, including elegy, religious meditation, the riddle, and epigrams such as 'Bede's Death Song'. As Kevin Crossley-Holland observes, in Anglo-Saxon poetry 'the lyric mood is always the elegiac' (*ibid*.: 46). The elegies collected in the *Exeter Book* (*circa* 940 CE) concern the loss of a lord, of loved ones, or the neglect and decay of great buildings that anticipates the later Romantic fascination with the fragment. In these elegiac poems, the natural world often stands in for human emotions. 'The Ruin' (eighth century CE), which surveys a site now considered to be the Roman city of Bath, prefigures the use of landscape in lyric poetry in the eighteenth and nineteenth centuries, where a speaker meditates on the religious, philosophical or emotional meaning of a geographical locale (see Chapter 4). Religious poems such as 'The Dream of the Rood' (ninth century CE) are similarly poised between a communal, homiletic mode of address, and a more meditative, internalised perspective. It blends an 'old' Germanic heroic world with Christianity, figuring Christ as the leader of a group of warriors, which includes the cross and the dreamer. Dream vision, widely deployed in medieval poetry, and prosopopoeia are used to vocalise the cross, the inanimate object on which the poem centres. As a visionary expression of faith, emphasising passionate feeling and vivid sensory experience, the poem inclines towards reverie, retreat and transcendence, features that constitute the touchstone of many modern definitions of lyric; yet it is simultaneously an invocation, an act of address. To anticipate a later discussion, if this lyric is 'overheard', it is overheard because the dreamer ventriloquises, listens to, or is addressed by an other: in this case, the cross.

The riddle is one of the most distinctive Anglo-Saxon poetic forms: most of Old English literature is full of mini-riddles, whether in Anglo-Saxon, Norse or Latin forms. The riddle is closely paralleled by the Old English kenning, a condensed, often oblique metaphor: the riddle is in effect 'an extended kenning' (*ibid.*: 236). The riddle epitomises the gradual shift in the history of lyric from oral to literate culture, from the rhythmic and musical towards the pictorial and abstract. Northrop Frye treats the riddle as a central form of *opsis*, one of the two basic modes of lyric poetry. *Opsis*, or 'doodle', relates to the visual element of lyric, while *melos*, or 'babble', is its musical aspect. Riddle brings together the visual and conceptual, and is 'intimately involved with the whole process of reducing language to visible form' (Frye 1957: 280). Anglo-Saxon riddles present a mental puzzle or paradox to be solved, and deal with a variety of subject matter: the fear of Viking raids, weaponry, aspects of the new Christian faith, sexual *double entendres*, and the celebration of objects, from chalices to churns, used either in religious ritual or in everyday working life. Daniel Tiffany has argued that it is possible to claim that lyric poetry first emerged in English as the 'enigmatic voice' (Tiffany 2001: 73) of these objects, which are depicted in cryptic or defamiliarising ways. This condensed metaphor illustrates not only the playful and highly reflexive nature of the riddle, but also implicitly acknowledges the move from speech to writing in the period:

> I watched four fair creatures
> travelling together; they left black tracks
> behind them. The support of the bird
> moved swiftly; it flew in the sky,
> dived under the waves. The struggling warrior
> continuously toiled, pointing out the paths
> to all four over the fine gold.
>
> (Crossley-Holland 1984: 243)

The 'solution' to this riddle is, of course, a pen and four fingers.

Through its striking and unexpected metaphorical comparisons, the riddle can be seen to anticipate the conceits of the metaphysical lyric in the seventeenth century. In more general terms, the riddle and many lyric poems share an intensity, economy and concentration of description. Andrew Welsh has argued that the riddle-maker and lyric poet deploy similar processes of elaboration and condensation, and illustrates this by comparing a native Canadian riddle that figures a man as a tree with Shakespeare's Sonnet 73:

> In Spring I am gay,
> In handsome array;
> In summer more clothing I wear;
> When colder it grows,
> I fling off my clothes;
> And in winter quite naked appear.
>
> (Welsh 1978: 33)

> That time of year thou mayst in me behold
> When yellow leaves, or none, or few, do hang
> Upon those boughs which shake against the cold,
> Bare ruined choirs where late the sweet birds sang.
>
> (Shakespeare 2006: 63)

Anglo-Saxon lyrics have only fragmentary existence in written form, and they relied primarily on oral transmission. They were copied down from oral sources in monastic scriptoria, and often transcribed in the margins of religious manuscripts. In some cases, their continued existence has been a matter of luck as much as careful preservation. The *Exeter Book*, a compilation of riddles, maxims and Christian poems, was given to the Cathedral by Leofric, the first Bishop of Exeter, but at various times it had to survive use as a cutting-board and the ravages of fire. The other main influence on medieval English poetry, the work of the troubadours in southern France in the twelfth and thirteenth centuries, and their counterparts, the *trouvères* of northern France, the *stilnovisti* in Italy, and the German *Minnesinger*, provides the most prominent instance of the move from oral to literate in medieval lyric. As Alan R. Press has pointed out, the troubadour tradition lies at the origin of lyric poetry throughout western Europe. The prominence of troubadour lyric does not arise purely from its repertoire of tropes and figures, variations on fixed formulae, or subject matter such as love, religious faith, or moral and political comment, but in its mix of musical and verbal harmonies, and in its bridging of the literary and the vernacular. The original language of the troubadour lyric is Provençal, or Occitan, a Romance tongue that emerged as an experimental literary language from the shadow of its 'parent Latin form' (Press 1971: 3). Troubadour poetry was intimately linked to the aristocratic world, but its forms, particularly *amour courtois*, with its elevated and spiritual discourse, were derived from popular songs. As the following observation by the troubadour poet Peire Vidal (active 1180–1206) suggests, lyric is perceived to be the possession of both 'high' and 'low' culture:

> All peoples, Christians, Jews, and Saracens, emperors, kings, princes, dukes, viscounts, barons, clerks burgesses, villeins, small and great continually set their minds on composing and singing, whether they wish themselves to compose, or to understand, or to recite, or to listen; so that scarcely can you be in a place so private or so solitary that you will not hear one or another, or all together, sing; for even the shepherds of the mountain have their greatest solace in singing. All the bad and the good in the world are kept in remembrance by poets, and you cannot find a word, be it well said or ill said, which is not held in remembrance, if once a poet has put it into rime; and poetry and song are the movers of all valorous deeds.
>
> (Whitmore 1918: 585)

In addition to his stress on the broad social appeal and relevance of the troubadour lyric, Vidal also implies the Pindaric function of the Provençal poem, even if it typically suggests interiority and introspection. Troubadour lyric is both commemorative and celebratory, and poetry and song are regarded as interdependent.

The troubadours performed their songs to different audiences, whether in courts, or in households of the feudal nobility. Both performer and audience were well aware that each song could assume a context specific to that setting, while remaining part of a recurrent thematic repertoire that would travel to another house. The transferable and stylised nature of troubadour lyrics, and their reinvention of generic formulae, means that they are 'unambiguously dramatic performances' (Lindley 1985: 53). Thus the troubadour poem at once relies upon recognisable formal conventions and upon the possibilities of context-specific improvisation and spontaneity. '*La douza votz ai auzida*' ('I have heard the sweet voice'), by Bernard de Ventadorn (active 1140–75), exemplifies this tension. It places the poetic persona within an emotional situation in which the conflict between the demands of the courtly ideal and the strength of the poet's feelings is dramatised. Here the love song is not the rendition of formulaic abstractions or an affirmation of the obligations of service, but a dramatic address in which the performance element can be foregrounded:

> *Mout l'avia gen servida*
> *Tro ac vas mi cor voltage;*
> *E pus ilh no m'es cobida,*
> *Mout sui fols si mais la ser.*
> I had most nobly served her, till she showed me a fickle heart; and
> since she's not accorded me, I'm a great fool if I serve her more.
>
> (Press 1971: 71)

The blend of 'high' and 'low', religious and secular forms and subject matter, and the interlinking of words, music and performance in Anglo-Saxon and troubadour poetry, established the pattern for medieval and early modern English lyric. Throughout the medieval period, lyric forms blur distinctions between literate art and popular cultural forms, and between elite and vernacular tongues. Medieval lyric operated in three languages, Latin, Anglo-Norman French and English: the educated poet was proficient in all three, and thus spanned the language of the clergy, the nobility and the lower strata of feudal society. The transmission and survival of medieval lyrics exemplify this formal and social intermingling. Many collections of lyrics that remain originally belonged to religious houses or to individual clergy, but a number survived in the commonplace books of laymen. The repertoire of the travelling singer–poet included secular and religious poems, ballads and carols, and perhaps the most famous collection, the Harley lyrics, consists of secular poems influenced by both Latin religious verse and the troubadours.

The recording and cataloguing of this repertoire was an uncertain process. Folk songs were transmitted and preserved orally, as parchment was expensive and cheaper alternatives such as wax tablets were less durable. Poems on religious themes were more likely than popular lyrics to be written down, and clerics would be less likely to record secular poems and songs (Davies 1963: 32). Yet secular forms were often adapted for sacred purposes. For example, many songs in praise of the Virgin Mary imitate the troubadour tradition of courtly love, as we shall see in greater detail in Chapter 5 when we consider lyrics that express sexual and spiritual desire. The early fourteenth century 'Maiden in the mor lay' was deemed by the Bishop of Ossory, Richard de Ledrede, unsuitable for the clergy to sing, yet he recast the poem into a Christian symbolic landscape. The young woman exposed to the elements becomes Mary, who awaits Christ's coming in the wilderness of the world, and she drinks cold water from 'the welle-spring' that denotes God's grace. Nonetheless, the elements of repetition and incantation, which suggest audience participation, suggest the poem's origins in popular folksong (*ibid.*: 321).

Medieval lyrics thus appealed in different ways to different social groups and, with their frequent combination of music and dance, often invited communal participation. Douglas Gray has stressed how lyric did not inhabit a rarefied and remote aesthetic realm, but fulfilled 'an integral part of the religious life of contemporary society':

> The lyrics are sometimes put to what we might recognize as 'literary' uses (e.g. in plays), but more often than not the impulse behind them is quite functional and practical. Utility is normally put before beauty, and sometimes, though fortunately not always, excludes it altogether. The lyrics were meant to be, and were, used, sometimes in private devotion and prayer, sometimes in public devotional display, sometimes to emphasize and drive home points in sermons.
>
> (Gray 1972: 37)

Medieval poetry was mainly anonymous and conventional in style and subject matter, and does not lend itself readily to notions of spontaneity and originality associated with the lyric since the Romantic period (Davies 1963: 20). Gray emphasises that modern definitions of lyric that lay stress on individual emotion are 'not applicable' to medieval poems, and this is particularly apparent in devotional lyrics. Medieval poets

> are not primarily concerned with the construction of an enduring object for other people to admire, but rather for other people to *use*. The medieval poet speaks not only for himself, but in the name of the many; if he uses the poetic 'I' it will be in a way which may be shared by his readers. It is a poetic stance which cannot be accurately described either as 'personal' or 'impersonal'.
>
> (Gray 1972: 60)

While the development of literary culture from the medieval to the early modern follows a broad trajectory from oral to manuscript to print, there are strong continuities between the periods in terms of complicated structures of address, the interweaving of religious and secular forms, and the strong element of performance. The intimate connection between words and music, and the devotional, commemorative and celebratory functions of lyric remain. Equally, the use of dramatic presentation and adoption of personae, inherited from the troubadours, influences early modern lyric forms. Many of the forms and conventions of medieval lyric are central to English poetry in the sixteenth and seventeenth centuries: the love song, the epideictic poem that praises a sovereign, patron or lover, and religious lyrics. Lyrics in the sixteenth and seventeenth centuries are often written to be performed to the accompaniment of music, but there is a gradual dissociation of song and lyric poetry in the period. This is partly a result of the development of print culture, and partly a consequence of the increasing concentration on the individual. Furniss and Bath observe that this philosophical focus on the unique self is reflected in 'a similar development in the lyric's potential for expressing individual selfhood, which was also largely unprecedented, in the poetry of this period' (Furniss and Bath 1996: 165). In the sixteenth century, poems were circulated privately in manuscript form at court or among groups of friends, rather than being intended to appear anonymously in print. The emphasis of privately circulated poetry in the Tudor period 'is much less upon the declaration of self, much more upon the exhibition of an artful mastery of language and idea' (Lindley 1985: 59). Lindley cites Philip Sidney's sonnet sequence *Astrophil and Stella* (1591) as an example of how this mode of transmission allows the poet to play with authorial identity: the sonnets are dependent to some extent on a personal frame of reference – the 'real' Stella is Lady Penelope Rich – but they are not the kind of transparent, 'sincere' utterances that are customarily associated with lyric since the Romantic period (Lindley 1985: 60). The relationship between writer and poetic persona, real life and poetic text, is implied but veiled in the sequence, which plays a knowing game with its first readers, who are well aware of Sidney's relationship with Rich.

While the early modern lyric becomes increasingly privatised in terms of distribution and reception, however, the dialogical and performance elements established in the medieval period remain. The close connection between selfhood and display took on acute social and political significance for the Tudor court. Lyric poetry, along with dancing and music, was a means of self-display through which the ambitious courtier could advance his political career. Francis Palgrave could treat Elizabethan lyric poems as the high point in the Golden Age of literary accomplishment, regarding them as 'treasures which might lead us in higher and healthier ways than those of the world' (Palgrave 1964: xxi). Yet far from representing the efflorescence of incomparable genius, the Renaissance lyric style could be learned, or emulated. William Tottel's *Miscellany* (1557), dedicated 'to the honor of the Englishe tong', represented a form of training guide for the gentleman who aspired to profess his poetic skill at court. Poetry became, in effect, 'a species of conduct' (Greenblatt 1980: 136). At once high-flown and practical, innocent and knowing, the lyric constituted a diverting exercise in wit and rhetorical skill and an instrument in the pursuit and service of power. As with the medieval lyric, the early modern lyric presupposes, and seeks to address, an audience. Gary Waller comments that lyric poems in the period 'assume a multiplicity of audiences' in their deployment of a variety of rhetorical techniques, and this is particularly marked 'in the way the lyric "I" invites a reader or hearer to become part of the poem's experience' (Waller 1993: 105).

The different ways in which the poetic voice is constructed underscore the late-medieval and Renaissance conception of texts as rhetorical performances rather than expressions of authentic emotions (Spiller 1992: 7). Lyric poets must adopt convincing postures and deploy conventions skilfully, in order to persuade the listener (or, in print, the implied reader) of the poet's apparent sincerity and strength of feeling, or to demonstrate wit and stylistic accomplishment. As Lindley observes, the Renaissance lyric 'is rarely, if ever, the voice "talking to itself or to nobody"': it is always a directed, rhetorical performance (Lindley 1985: 64). In *The Arte of English Poesie* (1589) George Puttenham reveals the multiple, and to some extent conflicting, purposes of lyric forms:

> The first founder of all good affections is honest love, as the mother of all the vicious is hatred. It was not therefore without reason that so commendable, yea honourable thing as love well meant, were it in. Princely estate or private, might in all civil common wealths be uttered in good forme and order as other laudable things are. And because love is of all other humane affections the most puissant and passionate, and most generall to all sortes and ages of men and women, so as whether it be of the yong or old or wise or holy, or high estate or low, none ever could truly bragge of any exemption in that case: it requireth a forme of Poesie variable, inconstant, affected, curious and most witty of any others ... with a thousand delicate

devises, odes, songs, elegies, ballads, sonets and other ditties, mooving one way and another to great compassion.

(Spiller 1992: 81–82)

Here the lyric is a product of artifice, able to deploy 'delicate devises' in the service of persuasion and entertainment, a mode fitted to the 'passionate' expression of 'private' feeling yet one that can fulfil its function in civil society. As Michael Spiller stresses, sonnets and other lyric forms identified by Puttenham are products of rhetoric, a matter of reason rather than passion, placing intellectual rather than emotional demands upon the recipient. Thus the sonnet's 'expressive function' cannot be discounted, but 'it is wholly subordinate to the persuasive function of poetry' (*ibid*.: 82).

Nonetheless, a more 'personal', meditative, intimate strand of lyric begins to feature more prominently in the period, as an increasing number of poems project a distinctively individualised voice that appears to speak from personal experience. In part, this is the result of a changing relationship between the writer and the court, and between the speaker and auditor of a lyric poem. In the seventeenth century, the figure of the professional poet emerges: poetry is no longer the preserve of the courtier or the fashionable amateur. The lyric begins to shift away from the exhibition of ingenuity and formal skill, towards the construction of a persona that is masked, ironically distanced or self-dramatised. This persona is distinct from the roles adopted by the balladeer or the court poet, and is epitomised by the speakers in John Donne's poetry; the directness and 'sincerity' of the speaker's utterance in poems such as 'The Good Morrow' are discussed at some length in the next chapter. This counter-tendency eventually led in the late eighteenth century to a distinct conceptual break with the 'persuasive' definition of the lyric mode. The paradigmatic shift in the Romantic period is from 'neo-classical rhetorical criteria' to a concern with intensity of feeling, interiority, and brevity (Lindley 1990: 193–94). Lindley argues that the distinctions drawn by a post-Romantic aesthetic between lyric and narrative, and between the poet speaking as him/herself and speaking through a persona, would have been unrecognisable to a medieval or early modern writer (*ibid*.: 194). As the next section demonstrates, however, the

Romantic break from previous accounts of the lyric is far from complete, whatever the declarations of its proponents.

GETTING PERSONAL: THE LYRIC 'I'

If we recall W. B. Sedgewick's evocation of the abiding and exemplary nature of ancient Greek lyric earlier in this chapter, his emphasis on directness, simplicity, spontaneity and rapture reveals a set of post-Romantic assumptions that are in sharp contrast to most classical and Renaissance definitions of lyric. These competing notions of rhetorical and rapturous lyric to some extent derive from the different conceptions of dialogue and performance in the Pindaric and Aristotelian models. Since the Romantic period, the dominant understanding of lyric has postulated an isolated speaker abstracted from specific historical conditions who can convey an immediacy of experience, 'personal' thoughts and feelings. As Barbara Hardy puts it, '[l]yric poetry isolates feeling in small compass and so renders it at its most intense ... the advantage of lyric in itself is its concentrated and patterned expression of feeling' (Hardy 1977: 1). The 'advantage of lyric poetry', Hardy argues, 'comes from its undiluted attention to feeling and feeling alone, and its articulateness in clarifying that feeling, in attesting conviction or what may somewhat misleadingly be called sincerity, and transferring this from privacy to publicity' (*ibid*.: 2). Lyric can 'speak in a pure, lucid, and intense voice': it is not a discursive mode, but it can speak about feelings. In Shakespeare's sonnets, for example, individual lyrics are intense expressions of 'moments of feeling', even if the whole sequence implies a buried narrative (*ibid*.: 3).

The Romantic lyric, with its emphasis on interiority, has become the dominant model for the modern lyric. It enacts a shift from the pronominal ('I/You') to a meditative inward turn in which the poet 'now talks to himself or to no one about his experience' (Johnson 1982: 7). John Ruskin declares in *Fors Clavigera* that 'lyric poetry is the expression by the poet of his own feelings' (Fowler 1982: 137). In 'What is Poetry?' (1833), John Stuart Mill presents poetry as self-communing and introspective, rather than a form of utterance concerned to locate an audience. In characterising the nature of this utterance, Mill distinguishes between poetry and eloquence:

> Poetry and eloquence are both alike the expression or utterance of feeling: but ... we should say that eloquence is *heard*; poetry is *over-heard*. Eloquence supposes an audience. The peculiarity of poetry appears to us to lie in the poet's utter unconsciousness of a listener. Poetry is feeling confessing itself to itself in moments of solitude ... Poetry, accordingly, is the natural fruit of solitude and meditation; eloquence, of intercourse with the world.
>
> (Mill 1973: 80–81)

Northrop Frye later reiterates Mill's terms by declaring that lyric is 'preeminently the utterance that is overheard', and by stressing the intimate connection lyric has with 'dream or vision, the individual communing with himself' (Frye 1957: 249, 250). This solitary, self-communing figure is evoked by Shelley in his 'A Defence of Poetry':

> A poet is a nightingale, who sits in darkness and sings to cheer its own solitude with sweet sounds; his auditors are as men entranced by the melody of an unseen musician, who feel that they are moved and softened, yet know not whence or why.
>
> (Shelley 2002: 512)

The emphases on unmediated emotion and the privatised, 'over-heard' nature of lyric are reinforced by the notion of its 'sincerity', which contrasts sharply with the self-conscious artifice of Eliza-bethan court poetry. This view is given exemplary articulation by Walter Blair and W. K. Chandler in 1935: 'Lyrical poetry arouses emotion because it expresses the author's feeling' (Hosek and Parker 1985: 240). In *The Lyric Impulse*, C. Day Lewis asserts that the essential spirit of lyric poetry produces 'a poem which expresses a single state of mind, a single mood, or sets two simple moods one against the other'. This poetry is 'simple, pure, trans-parent, impersonal after the best lyric model' (Day Lewis 1965: 3, 144–45). In spite of the shared assumptions about lyric as a translucent, intensely felt, individual utterance, the distance between Blair and Chandler's sense of lyric as an outpouring of private feeling, and Day-Lewis's emphasis on the pure, impersonal quality of the ideal lyric betrays an underlying uncertainty about the identity of the speaker or persona in a lyric poem. As Elisabeth A. Howe observes, while the lyric does not necessarily represent the thoughts or feelings of the poet, it 'also does not represent anyone else'. This makes lyric poems distinct from the dramatic monologue: 'A characteristic feature of the lyric "I" is precisely this vagueness that allows the reader to equate it with the poet, perhaps; to identify with it himself, or herself; or to see it as a universal "I" belonging to no-one and to everyone' (Howe 1996: 6). Such vagueness enables Sharon Cameron to claim that the lyric 'is a departure ... from the finite constructions of identity', fore-grounding a speaker whose 'origin remains deliberately unspecified' (Cameron 1979: 208). In view of the forms that lyric poetry has conventionally taken, it would seem hard to demur from Barbara Hernstein Smith's observation that 'lyric poems typically repre-sent personal utterances' (Smith 1978: 8); yet the nature of that 'personal utterance' is a crucial matter in definitions of the lyric. Many accounts of the lyric mode set out to strongly qualify, or demystify, this stress on the 'personal' or 'private'.

The emphasis on the self-communing, unfettered 'I' has laid lyric open to materialist critiques of its conservatism and ahis-toricism. As Theodor Adorno observes: 'The "I" whose voice is heard in the lyric is an "I" that defines and expresses itself as something opposed to the collective, to objectivity; it is not immediately at one with the nature to which its expression refers' (Adorno 1974: 41). The ideal of lyric poetry 'is to remain unaffected by bustle and commotion', and the lyric work 'hopes to attain universality through unrestrained individuation' (*ibid.*: 37, 38) This uni-versality is, however, 'social in nature', since 'the lyric work of art's withdrawal into itself, its self-absorption, its detachment from the social surface, is socially motivated behind the author's back' (*ibid.*: 43). Adorno concludes that lyric is most socially grounded when it communicates nothing, when it does not chime with society. Hugh Grady follows Adorno's approach by highlighting the limitations of some Marxist approaches that have applied the techniques of analysis appropriate to the novel and drama, in the desire 'to find in individual poems the reflection of sociohistoric forces and conflicts'. This is because the traditional preoccupations of lyric (love, death, nature, transcendence) seem resistant to materialist approaches and appear more amenable to 'purely formalist approaches' (Grady 1981: 544). Grady argues that the lyric is not merely a mirror of society; instead, 'in the lyric, bourgeois society attempts to confront what it is not' (*ibid.*: 551). It is a projective, speculative aesthetic form, and its putative 'retreat' from the social world can be read as affirmative rather than reactive. The lyric becomes the 'specialized literary genre for Utopian vision ... We could say that the lyric is a reflection of social conditions, but only as a photographic negative is a reflection. The lyric seeks to reverse the registers of reality as it now exists. It is an expression and formulation of the human impulse to Utopia' (*ibid.*: 551).

Grady traces both the 'negative' reflection of modernity and the utopic impulse in Coleridge's 'Kubla Khan' (1797–98). The poem marks a move away from rationalist discourse into self-reflexiveness: 'It is the otherness of the poem that bids for our comprehension; the poem is anything but a mirror of reality' (*ibid.*: 555). In these materialist accounts, lyric is presented as a dialogical, engaged (or indirectly engaged) poetic form rather than as one that privileges abstraction and timelessness. The lyric might instead be termed untimely, in the sense of its imagining of different historical and conceptual possibilities, and its reading against the prevailing ideological grain. The voice or subjectivity it constructs is not self-communing, and its overheard utterance does not exist in an eternal present. Within the framework of this argument, the lyric self can be seen as historically situated, a self that speaks, albeit often in muted form, to the moment.

The stress on sincerity, feeling and intimate expression also tends to overlook the irreducible problem that the lyric self who speaks is a linguistic construct. As Antony Easthope emphasises, the subjectivity that lyric presents 'must be approached not as the point of origin but as the effect of a poetic discourse' (Easthope 1983: 31). Thus lyric cannot be regarded as presenting the unmediated, spontaneous 'effusion of genius' that for John Henry Newman, in his 1829 essay 'Poetry with Reference to Aristotle's

Poetics', constituted true poetry (Wimsatt and Brooks 1970: 435). As Jonathan Culler stresses: 'The poetic persona is a construct, a function of the language of the poem, but it nonetheless fulfils the unifying role of the individual subject, and even poems which make it difficult to construct a poetic voice rely for their effects on the fact that the reader will try to construct an enunciative posture' (Culler 1975: 170). It is the reader, responding to the linguistic effects of the text, who makes the 'I' speak in a lyric poem. As such, the lyric speaker is a fiction, albeit perhaps a necessary fiction. Lyric makes the 'I' seem familiar, a confidant, a recognisable interlocutor, and usually appears to present a stable, consistent point of view. Yet at the same time, the reader of a lyric poem must constantly ask: 'who is speaking/ observing/ remembering/ reflecting/ meditating/ exhorting/ praising/ imagining here? How is she/he (or sometimes it) addressing me now, at this time?' As we shall see in subsequent chapters, the lyric 'I' is often an enigmatic, inconsistent figure or anchoring point in a poetic text. We can read lyric as an intensely self-reflexive poetic form in a double sense: it is a self-conscious reflection on the relationship of poetry, subjectivity and voice, and it often produces uncertain or contradictory constructions of the self. This is particularly marked in some strands of twentieth- and twenty-first-century poetry, as Chapter 4 will show. As the next section demonstrates, the way in which this 'I' speaks, its mode of address, has been an abiding preoccupation in definitions of lyric.

SPEAKING OF LYRIC: VOICE AND ADDRESS

Lyric practice has by now become almost entirely separated from song and music, but nonetheless lyric has continued to be defined in terms of voice and dramatised presentation from antiquity to the present. As we saw earlier in the chapter, many types of lyric were put to ceremonial or display purposes in ancient Greece and Rome, a practice that continued into the early modern period. By using the example of the Roman poet Catullus (*circa* 84–54 BCE), W. R. Johnson identifies three categories of pronominal address that apply to lyric practice from its classical origins to the present: I–You poems, where the poet addresses, or pretends to address, thoughts and feelings to another person; meditative poems, where the poet speaks to him- or herself or to no-one, and sometimes apostrophises the dead, abstract concepts or non-human entities; and dramatic monologues, dialogues or narratives, where the poet is absent from the presentation (Johnson 1982: 3). The varying conditions of transmission and reception, and the different expectations of poet and audience, in the history of the lyric have produced quite distinctive manifestations of both the poetic persona and the mode of address. A troubadour playing to his aristocratic hosts, a poet circulating a poem in manuscript form among a small circle of associates, and a singer performing in a communal setting clearly provide different experiences from the relatively private, 'anonymous' reading of a printed poem.

In spite of these changing contexts, however, the 'oral convention' (Hosek and Parker 1985: 16) has remained a staple component in definitions of lyric. Although modern poetic theory has tended to subdue the neoclassical emphasis on rhetoric, persuasion and argument, it has continued to stress the dramatic nature of lyric utterance and promote the fiction of a speaking self. Paul de Man acknowledges the dominance of this 'oral' fiction in literary criticism: 'The principle of intelligibility, in lyric poetry, depends on the phenomenalization of the poetic voice. Our claim to understand a lyric text coincides with the actualization of a speaking voice, be it (monologically) that of the poet or (dialogically) that of the exchange that takes place between the author and reader in the process of comprehension' (de Man 1985: 55). The majority of modern accounts of lyric speech are heavily influenced by Mill's notion of the 'overheard' utterance. Lyrics are seen to position us in the presence of a real speaker who acts in character, usually oblivious to an auditor. The addressee is often absent or, at best, implied; the reader/listener must eavesdrop or identify imaginatively with the speaker or the addressee. To deploy Johnston's model, the modern lyric is the apotheosis of meditative verse, and the near-disappearance of the lyric 'you'. (The following two chapters interrogate this sense of a gradual 'inward turn' in the history of lyric.)

Just as debates about the function and value of lyric hark back to antiquity, attempts to theorise the lyric speaker also draw on classical precedents. For Plato and Aristotle, poetry is very much a matter of 'public' speaking and dramatic performance. In *The*

Republic, Plato delineates the various voices of poetry: the voice of the poet speaking for himself, as in choral songs (lyric) or 'dithyrambs'; the imitated voice of dramatic characters, speaking in dialogue in forms such as tragedy; and the voice of epic poetry, in which the poet narrates in his own voice, but also represents or imitates voices of characters speaking in their own voices (Plato 1987: 91–93). T. S. Eliot's essay 'The Three Voices of Poetry' (1953) mirrors and modifies Plato's tripartite structure. Each of these voices becomes progressively more dramatic:

> The first voice is the voice of the poet talking to himself – or to nobody. The second is the voice of the poet addressing an audience, whether large or small. The third is the voice of the poet when he attempts to create a dramatic character speaking in verse; when he is saying, not what he would say in his own person, but only what he can say within the limits of one imaginary character addressing another imaginary character.
>
> (Eliot 1990: 89)

Although Eliot argues that 'in every poem, from the private meditation to the epic or the drama, there is more than one voice to be heard' (*ibid.*: 100), he identifies lyric poetry primarily with the 'first' voice. Eliot's description of this first voice echoes Mill's 'overheard' lyric, but he portrays it as a more radical and unsettling mode of address. The lyric is an unconscious or involuntary utterance, in which the poet 'is oppressed by a burden which he must bring to birth in order to obtain relief'. The lyric poem is an 'exorcism' of this 'demon', and its completion constitutes a moment 'of exhaustion, of appeasement, of absolution, and of something very near annihilation, which is in itself indescribable' (*ibid.*: 98). The lyric voice is not a form of conscious expression or communication: rather, it emerges from an obscure, agonistic process that involves the removal or obliteration of the self. It is as if words speak through the poet, or through the unspecified voice of the lyric poem.

While the assumed presence of a speaker or a voice – 'fictional' or sincere, a persona or 'overheard' figure – has become commonplace in most definitions of modern lyric, the nature of address has been a source of critical dispute. There are two opposing ways of viewing lyric in terms of its situation and mode of address: it can be expressive and self-dramatising, or it can be rhetorical, argumentative and persuasive (Winters 1957). The former definition has dominated in twentieth-century poetic practice, and in critical accounts of lyric. For example, Charles Whitmore notes approvingly that 'lyric tends to subdue the emphasis on rhetorical effect, and the diversion of poetry to non-poetical purposes'. In this rejection of rhetoric and persuasion, 'lyric has an intimate association with the essence of poetry' (Whitmore 1918: 589). Lyric diction 'must be of the choicest, selected with the utmost desire to secure harmony and suggestiveness' (*ibid.*: 598). Whitmore's dual emphasis on harmony and suggestiveness anticipates the later stress on unity of form and content in New Criticism, and on ambiguity as the defining feature of the language of poetry. The work of the American New Critics, such as Cleanth Brooks, W. K. Wimsatt and John Crowe Ransom, in the 1940s and 1950s opposed the notion of an expressive, Romantic lyric that emphasised sincerity and direct feeling. In 'The Intentional Fallacy' (1946), Wimsatt and Monroe C. Beardsley argue that literary criticism does not involve a search for the author's intentions, since knowledge of these is 'neither available nor desirable' (Wimsatt 1970: 3). The proper object of critical study is the literary text, not the biographical author, and questions of 'spontaneity' and 'authenticity' are secondary to qualities such as 'integrity' and 'unity' (*ibid.*: 9). For New Criticism, a poem's ambiguity expresses and enhances the richness and complexity of its content, and critical interpretation can resolve its ambiguities into an organic whole. Thus ambiguity is not an example of the inherent slipperiness and contradiction of language, but is a guarantee of the poem's, if not the poet's, sincerity of intent.

While figures such as C. Day Lewis continued to affirm the purity and simplicity of lyric poetry – 'irony and complexity of meaning are wholly foreign to the lyric' (Day Lewis 1961: 2) – the New Critical method became dominant in the reading and teaching of poetry for a large part of the later twentieth century. Its characteristic approach is to construct or imagine the context in which we encounter the lyric persona, to identify the tone of voice in which that persona addresses us, and thus to infer the state of mind, preoccupations and attitudes of the speaker. Thus the reader can stabilise the ambiguity of a poem and achieve interpretative closure. For New Criticism, all poems are implied dramatic monologues. (The dramatic monologue is discussed at length in Chapter 4.) Cleanth Brooks and Robert Penn Warren stress that a poem can be a 'little drama', obliging us to develop a sense of the speaker's identity (Brooks and Penn Warren 1976: 13–14). More fundamentally, each poem is an utterance, with a speaker, a 'provocation to utterance', and an audience; this is true not only of poems in which characters speak, such as dramatic monologues, but also of 'the most lyrical piece'. Even in a meditative lyric poem, there is an audience: 'what is of obvious importance is the attitude toward the subject, toward what has provoked the utterance' (*ibid*.: 112–13). For Wimsatt and Brooks, 'the briefest lyric ... has a focus or an aim ... the most fragile lyric has at least one character, that of the implied speaker himself, and it has a "plot" – an arrangement of psychic incidents, with a development, at least of mood' (Wimsatt and Brooks 1965: 691). In Brooks's terms, our attention to the speaker's utterance will disclose 'the total and governing attitude' of the lyric (Brooks 1968: 207). Benedetto Croce's 1937 definition for the *Encyclopedia Britannica* strikingly affirms the notion of the lyric's essentially dramatic nature: 'The lyric is not a pouring forth; it is not a cry or a lament; it is an objectification in which the ego sees itself on the stage, narrates itself, and dramatizes itself; and this lyrical spirit forms the poetry both of epic and of drama, which are therefore distinguished from the lyric only by external signs' (Wimsatt and Brooks 1965: 510). The resistance to the expressive lyric 'cry' in this definition is clear: Croce steers a path between the oratory associated with the Pindaric and the pure introspection of Mill's 'overheard' lyric.

As Culler has argued, the New Critical theory of the lyric does not readily fit lyrics whose voice is not individualised, such as songs, poems in the 'bardic' tradition or apostrophes. The apostrophe is a poem that directly addresses abstractions, absent or quasi-divine presences in a tone of speech that is often strange or unsettling (Culler 1985: 40). It can invoke ideas and states of mind (immortality, melancholy, dejection), the natural world (skylarks, nightingales, roses), or the dead. Apostrophe is 'embarrassing', because it is often self-consciously poetical and grandiloquent: it problematises the attempt to treat lyric poems as dramatic monologues. It is relatively straightforward for the reader to infer an attitude from meditative poems such as 'Tintern Abbey' or 'This Lime-Tree Bower My Prison', which appear to convey a memory, or present a coherent reflection. It is less easy to treat apostrophes as 'fictional representations of plausible historical utterances' (*ibid.*: 39), or the 'overheard' lyric utterance postulated by Mill. Yet apostrophe is such a common feature of lyric that it is almost possible 'to identify apostrophe with lyric itself' (Culler 1981: 137). In Culler's view, to understand the poetics of the lyric we should study apostrophe: apostrophes illustrate that lyric can involve an estranging rather than an engaging or familiar voice, and that its mode of address does not necessarily conform to a conventional sender/receiver model of communication.

Culler cites Keats's apostrophic poem 'This Living Hand' (1819) in order to question established conceptions of lyric. The 'now' of apostrophe is 'not a moment in a temporal sequence but a *now* of discourse, of writing'. The lyric is typically treated as 'a monument to immediacy', but for Culler this immediacy is 'detemporalized ... a fictional present in which nothing happens but which is the essence of happening' (*ibid.*: 152). This differs from the New Critical emphasis on lyric presenting a dramatic situation. Apostrophe is a form of lyric that does not constitute an isolated dramatic moment within a larger surrounding narrative or sequence of events. 'This Living Hand' inhabits a time and space and yet seeks to remain outside those constraints, and asks the reader to do the same:

> This living hand, now warm and capable
> Of earnest grasping, would, if it were cold
> And in the icy silence of the tomb,
> So haunt thy days and chill thy dreaming nights
> That thou would wish thine own heart dry of blood
> So in my veins red life might stream again,
> And thou be conscience-calmed – see here it is –
> I hold it towards you.
>
> (Keats 1977: 459)

It is all too easy to commit the intentional fallacy, to read this poem as one of Keats's last, autobiographical statements: yet the text *is* concerned with survival. The poem asks its future recipient – the apostrophic addressee – to perform an act of prosopopoeia, the act of giving a voice to the dead. Paul de Man has argued that there is a close relationship between apostrophes that address the dead and prosopopoeia: the dead are given voice and, by the same logic, the living 'are struck dumb, frozen in their own death' (de Man 1984: 78).

'This Living Hand' positions the reader as both object and subject of the lyric utterance: we are invited to grant life and warmth to the icy hand, but doing so leaves us suspended between past and present, the inanimate and the animate. We are thus obliged to identify with an 'I' who is in, and out of, time. Wimsatt and Brooks cite Kenneth Burke's observation that the essence of lyric is a *state of arrest*, and it is 'the dialectical counterpart of action'; the special aptitude of lyric is for 'conveying a state of mind, for erecting a moment into a universe' (Wimsatt and Brooks 1965: 697). Yet we might argue that Keats's poem illustrates Andrew Welsh's observation that 'the sense of time caught in space form[s] a complex which lies at the root of lyric poetry' (Welsh 1978: 64). The poem does not turn 'a moment into a universe': the reader is arrested by the invitation to clasp an outstretched hand, and is caught in a moment of time when something *might happen*.

The reader is both recipient and instigator of the act of address, and only she or he can perform the act it describes and demands: it asks the reader to *do* something. Richard Bradford terms lyric the most prominent form of poetic speech act – an act that names, commands, promises, declares, invokes – as the hearer is directly addressed and drawn into the context of the utterance (Bradford 1993: 213). This is in marked contrast to Mill's sense of lyric as an involuntary, spontaneous or 'unconscious' utterance. 'This Living Hand' can be read as a self-sufficient mini-drama presenting the thoughts and attitudes of a persona, and the reader/listener is an eavesdropper rather than an implied participant in the 'action', its timeless moment of reflection on (im)mortality. Its dialogue is internalised, and abstracted from any larger story or context (which we are obliged to invent). But it is, at the same time, a speech act, an appeal to an unnamed, even unforeseeable other in the future. As an apostrophe, the poem is not just speaking 'about' something: it is a speaking 'to' that requests or demands a response, an action, from its addressee. It draws attention to the moment of its performance, the issuing of its injunction and its anticipated reception, at least as much as it presents an isolated dramatic situation. We can thus treat the lyric as a performative utterance in the manner outlined by the philosopher J. L. Austin's speech–act theory (Austin 1962). A performative is a statement – a demand, a promise, an appeal or a curse – that has the capacity both to *say* and *do*, to *describe* and also *perform* an action. 'This Living Hand' is performative, but what it *does* to us as readers is not certain; its performance cannot be managed or contained in the way that New Criticism would tame the 'open' ambiguity of the text. The 'drama' of Keats's poem takes place in the here and now, the moment of reading, the moment of responding to the text's plea, invitation or exhortation. It casts a mimetic spell that attempts to present the reality and sincerity of the speaker's plea, yet simultaneously shows its artificiality. For Culler, lyric constantly strives for this complex play of mystification and demystification (Culler 1981: 154). To identify in some fashion with the speaker, we have to live out the fiction and remain in a perpetual moment of possibility. It is as if lyric says, as proof of its authenticity: 'Here you have it, in writing. The lyric moment is right here, right now, in front of you. Just reach out and embrace it.'

So 'This Living Hand', in many ways the epitome of the Romantic and post-Romantic lyric, has a rhetorical, persuasive dimension, even if it cannot 'see' its audience or addressee. To an extent, the poem illustrates W. R. Johnson's contention that '[w]hat is essential ... to lyric is rhetoric' (Johnson 1982: 23). In its strange detachment, however, it also corresponds to Tzvetan Todorov's sense of a 'non-representational' text, the 'most obvious' case of which is that of a kind of poetry, usually called lyrical, which does not describe events, which evokes nothing that is external to itself' (Todorov 1990: 48). In conventional chronological terms, it is poised between 'early' and 'later' lyric. Yet, as this chapter has argued, the definition of lyric from classical antiquity onwards has not been merely a matter of progressive development from, say, external to internal, public to private, or popular to elite. This chapter has briefly surveyed the changing forms that lyric has taken, the widely varying historical contexts in which it has operated, the differing valuations ascribed to it, and the transformations in its prominence and functions. In spite of these changes, however, attempts to define lyric have centred consistently on its modes of address, and the nature of its addressee. We have seen lyric construed, and practised, as an anonymous, didactic, conventional literary mode; as a product of self-conscious artifice and often formulaic convention; as a matter of performance and display; and as an integral part of everyday life. We have also seen lyric categorised at a later moment as introspective, rarefied and sincere, as an 'overheard' utterance of individual thoughts and feelings; and as a mode that stands apart from the everyday world. In effect, however, in each historical period, understandings of lyric have tended to negotiate between these different definitions. The following chapters show lyric to be concerned with both 'inner' and 'outer' worlds, and stress the recurrent importance of subjectivity and speaking voice in any examination of lyric.

3

LYRIC AND THE ART OF PERSUASION

The early modern period is marked by a great variety of lyric practices and definitions of lyric. This chapter begins by discussing the major influence of the Petrarchan tradition on English lyric in the sixteenth century. The courtly lyric is characterised by rhetorical display rather than 'personal' feeling, and it also depends heavily upon a performance element. The chapter then considers more explicit versions of lyric performance, such as dramatic soliloquy and the metaphysical lyric of John Donne. (The central relationship between poetry and song in the Elizabethan period is examined in Chapter 6.) The chapter goes on to trace the development of the Ode, including the Horatian, the Pindaric, elegy and hymn, in the later seventeenth and eighteenth centuries, and ends by tracing the gradual move towards the Romantic conception of lyric in the later eighteenth century. Despite the differences between these forms of lyric, they consistently present a speaker who embarks on a process of persuasion.

In the previous chapter, we saw how the ritual and communal functions of mainly anonymous medieval lyrics offered a sharp contrast to later ideas of an individual consciousness that speaks through the poem. As Lindley argues, the modern distinctions between lyric and narrative, and between the poet speaking 'directly' and the poet speaking through a persona, would have been unrecognisable to medieval and early modern poets. In the early modern period, the notion of an unmediated lyric voice speaking is also largely absent: the 'personal' voice of the lyric is explicitly a product of rhetorical devices. As Stephen Greenblatt has argued, rather than developing a unique or inimitable poetic voice, court poets are 'as much written by their conventional lyric as writers of them' (Greenblatt 1980: 139). Lyric practice, and the construction of a poetic voice by poets trained in rhetoric, such as Wyatt and Donne, is governed by 'a habit of mind which saw language as an instrument of persuasion, and poetry as a branch of epideictic rhetoric, a means of instruction through praise or blame' (Lindley 1990: 192). Renaissance poets have a clear sense of audience and conditions of address, and in almost all poetry of the period, 'there is a self-conscious, public dimension' (*ibid.*). While a modern idea of the self is clearly in formation in lyric texts of the sixteenth century, manuscripts circulated among small groups of friends, and poems were written in praise of patrons or influential figures and could function as a strategy for self-advancement.

While lyric was ascribed a serious role in the sixteenth and seventeenth centuries, it was also often regarded as a relatively minor poetic genre. Tottel's 1557 *Miscellany* provided a model for rival collections in the Tudor period, such as George Turberville's *Epigrams, Songs, Epitaphes and Sonets* (1567) and George Gascoigne's *A Hundredth Sundrie Flowers* (1573), which stressed the moral and civic aims rather than the metaphysical or psychological dimensions of lyric (Waller 1993: 81). Sir Philip Sidney's *An Apology for Poetry* (1595) emphasises the epideictic and morally instructive purposes of lyric: the lyric poet 'with his tuned lyre and well-accorded voice, giveth praise, the reward of virtue, to virtuous acts; gives moral precepts, and natural problems ... sometimes raiseth up his voice to the height of the heavens, in singing the lauds of the immortal God' (Sidney 1965: 118). In contrast, Puttenham's *The Arte of English Poetry* (1589) depicts lyric as the 'meanest sort' of poetry, 'used for recreation only' (Waller 1993: 70). In the seventeenth and early eighteenth centuries, lyric was subjected to similarly contradictory valuations. As we shall see later in this chapter, it was associated with 'higher' public forms, such as the ode, but many of its manifestations were relegated to the status of entertainment and diversion. Joshua Poole, writing in 1657, sees the lyric genre as encompassing 'Madrigals, Sonnets, Hymns, Ballets, Odes, whereof some are amorous, some rural, some military, some jovial, made for drollery and drinking' (Curran 1986: 24–25). In an echo of Aristotle's hierarchy, whereby lyric is an interlude in the drama and also subordinate to epic, Thomas Hobbes declares that lyrics 'are but essays and parts of an entire poem' (Whitmore 1918: 586).

Yet, as Gary Waller observes, the very qualities that left lyric at the bottom of Puttenham's poetic hierarchy in the late sixteenth century are precisely those that attract the modern reader to the poetry of Wyatt, Sidney, Donne and others. Schooled in close reading techniques deployed in the classroom, and influenced by the Romantic definition of lyric, readers now seize on shorter early modern poems for their privileging of passionate, exquisite personal feeling. These moments of poetic intensity and apparent intimacy prove an attractive alternative to longer poems such as *The Faerie Queene* and *Paradise Lost*, which present major challenges to the contemporary reader. Lyric in the period was perceived as the pastime of the amateur, and this apparent lack of seriousness would seem to confirm the habitual view of lyric as timeless and unworldly, remote from historical conflict. Yet it is the proximity of lyric to the major struggles for power in the sixteenth and seventeenth centuries – whether in the court, in wider political life, or in the religious conflicts of the period – that demands our attention. As Waller argues: 'Despite its apparent superficiality and marginal social role the lyric was uncannily able to articulate the significance of the complex relations between language and power, literary text and social text' (Waller 1993: 73).

THE COURTLY LYRIC

The Tudor court in England, and the Scottish court of James IV, were highly artificial worlds of display, dissembling and ornate praise, where the courtier had to negotiate the vagaries of patronage and political intrigue. Greenblatt identifies this as a moment in which 'there appears to be an increased self-consciousness about the fashioning of human identity as a manipulable, artful process' (Greenblatt 1980: 2). The process of self-fashioning comprises 'the creation of literary characters, the shaping of one's own identity, the experience of being moulded by forces outside one's own control, the attempt to fashion other selves' (*ibid.*: 3). Thus the ambitious courtier had to fashion a flexible persona or 'self' that could survive and flourish in such a culture; in court poetry this heightened sensitivity to subjectivity was accompanied by an uncertainty about the nature of the individual voice of the poet. The court appropriated poetry as an instrument of political power. In such a context, the central lyric form of the period, the love poem, was not merely a vehicle for the expression of amorous desires and elevated, even abstract emotions: it was a device through which to make a social impression, or to gain political influence. The love lyric also implied that the poet had sufficient leisure 'to codify and refine' the different aspects of love (Parfitt 1992: 23). The work of the fourteenth-century Italian poet Petrarch provided a formal and philosophical framework within which Tudor court lyric could play out this tension between 'private' desire and social aspiration, inner depth and rhetorical performance, individuality and generic convention. The central form of the courtly lyric, particularly in the Petrarchan mode, is the sonnet. Similarly to the lyric mode, a 'terminological looseness' surrounded the sonnet form (Spiller 1992: 102). In Provençal and early Italian usage, a *sonet* or *sonetto* meant a short lyric poem, whereas in sixteenth- and seventeenth-century Britain the sonnet often denoted merely a light poem that was not necessarily seen as 'lyric'. Petrarch's *Canzoniere*, comprising more than 360 sonnets addressed to a woman named Laura (based on a real woman, probably Laura de Sade, who died in 1348), had established a poetic tradition in Italy, Spain and France by the time sonnets began to be imitated in England in the early sixteenth century.

Sir Thomas Wyatt (1503–42) is generally regarded as the first sonneteer in the English language; he was introduced to the form partly as the result of his diplomatic missions to Italy and France, and his adaptation of Petrarchan conventions to English culture in a variety of verse forms heavily influenced subsequent court poetry in the sixteenth century. The Petrarchan sonnet, which operates through antithesis and instability, and represents 'the perfection of momentary equilibrium' (Spiller 1992: 49), was ideally fitted to the rhetorical demands of court poetry. In the later Elizabethan period, Petrarchism became 'part of public policy' (Waller 1993: 80). The central features of the Petrarchan love poem – the changeability of the self, the investment of ornate rhetorical skill that cannot hope to produce an adequate return, the appeals to a remote object of veneration, and the dialectic of self-abasement and frustration – could be deployed to express the tension between the Tudor courtier's desire to please and flatter, and a countervailing impulse towards rhetorical persuasion. As in Petrarch's sonnets, the courtly lyric was a temporary resolution to social and psychological contradiction. The conflicting requirements of ornament and argument, entertainment and education demanded by life at court are precisely those conflicts that characterise definitions of lyric in the period.

Renaissance court culture revolved around the pursuit of reward and advancement, and there were clear parallels between the reigns of Catherine de Medici (regent of France 1560–74) and Elizabeth I. The court culture associated with both placed a premium on display and rhetorical skill, and promoted a Petrarchan poetics at whose mythological centre was a female figure of transcendent beauty and wisdom. The sense of extravagant striving for the favour of a remote, ethereal presence is exemplified by Sonnet 68 from Sidney's *Astrophil and Stella*:

> Stella, the onely Planet of my light,
> Light of my life, and life of my desire,
> Chief good, whereto my hope doth onely aspire,
> World of my wealth, and heav'n of my delight,
> Why doest thou spend the treasures of thy sprite
> With voice more fit to wed Amphion's lyre,
> Seeking to quench in me the noble fire
> Fed by thy worth, and kindled by thy sight?
> And all in vaine, for while thy breath most sweet,

With choisest words, the words with reasons rare,
Thy reasons firmly set on Vertue's feet,
Labour to kill in me this killing care,
O thinke I then, what paradise of joy
It is, so faire a Vertue to enjoy.
                                        (Sidney 1962: 200)

This tireless yearning seems less an appeal to a real woman than to a spiritual ideal. Stella's voice is likened to Amphion's lyre, which could charm stones to life: the poet's own lyre is deployed in the pursuit of his Lady's transfiguring power. The very unattainability of her 'Vertue' at once inspires and defeats the poet's 'killing care'. The strategy of the Petrarchan lover mirrors that of the aspiring courtier: the speaker admits weakness to solicit favour, and professes devotion in order to merit reward. This sonnet from Spenser's *Amoretti* (1595) reiterates the value of such suffering in more abstract terms:

Sweet is the rose, but grows upon a brere;
Sweet is the juniper, but sharp his bough;
Sweet is the eglantine, but pricketh near;
Sweet is the fir-bloom, but his branches rough;
Sweet is the cypress, but his rind is tough;
Sweet is the nut, but bitter is his pill;
Sweet is the broom-flower, but yet sour enough;
And sweet is moly, but his root is ill.
So every sweet with sour is tempered still,
That maketh it be coveted the more;
For easy things, that may be got at will,
Most sorts of men do set but little store.
Why then should I account of little pain,
That endless pleasure shall unto me gain?
                                        (Ault 1949: 204)

Service and endurance are their own reward, as pleasure is short-lived and 'every sweet with sour is tempered still'. The tempering of satisfaction merely generates more desire: there is no meaningful gain without pain, even if 'endless pleasure' is deferred to an unspecified future point. These sonnets outline the frustrations and uncertainties of the courtier's position. Like the courtly lover, the aspiring gentleman is loyal, a supplicant full of hope but fearful of rejection, dependent on the whims of patronage and prey to capricious changes of fortune, mindful of the thin line between success and failure. Above all, there is an acceptance of the game that must be played and the roles that must be performed in love, in poetry and in social conduct. In an unpredictable court, however, the courtier–poet assumed roles that were in part consciously fashioned, and in part imposed by circumstance. The career of Sir Walter Ralegh, a court favourite who became an imprisoned outcast under Elizabeth, is a striking example of the risks and possibilities of this dangerous game. Poems such as 'Praisd Be Dianas Faire and Harmless Light' and 'Ocean to Scinthia' demonstrate the different outcomes of this game. 'Praisd Be Dianas Faire and Harmless Light' overtly celebrates Elizabeth's majesty: 'Praisd be hir powre, by which all powres abound' (Waller 1993: 113). In stark contrast to this naked propaganda, 'Ocean to Scinthia' has the lover lamenting his 'twelve yeares' wasted in loyal service to a woman who has abandoned him (*ibid*.: 114).

In Wyatt's courtly lyrics, this 'game' of vain pursuit and aspiration can subside into bitterness and regret. His sonnet, 'Whoso List to Hunt' (discussed at length in Chapter 5) is, in part, an allegory of erotic desire prohibited by royal power. 'The Lover Showeth How He is Forsaken of Such as He Sometime Enjoyed', usually known as 'They Flee From Me', exemplifies the social and political pressures that shape the courtly lyric in the period:

> They flee from me that sometime did me seek,
> With naked foot stalking within my chamber:
> Once have I seen them gentle, tame, and meek,
> That now are wild, and do not once remember
> That sometime they have put themselves in danger
> To take bread at my hand: and now they range,
> Busily seeking in continual change.
>
> Thankèd be fortune, it hath been otherwise,
> Twenty times better; but once especial

In thin array, after a pleasant guise,
When her loose gown did from her shoulders fall,
And she me caught in her arms long and small,
And therewithal so sweetly did me kiss,
And softly said, 'Dear heart, how like you this?'

It was no dream; for I lay broad awaking:
But all is turned now, through my gentleness,
Into a bitter fashion of forsaking;
And I have leave to go of her goodness;
And she also to use new-fangleness.
But since that I unkindly so am servèd,
'How like you this' – what hath she now deservèd?

                                    (Ault 1949: 7–8)

The poem speaks the language of complaint, and dwells on the
fickleness of love and the struggle for ascendancy that underpins
erotic game-playing. There are none of the flourishes associated with
Spenser or Sidney. The text is also preoccupied with domination
and submission, aggression and compliance, all acute concerns for
those seeking power and advancement in the Tudor court. The
woman is seemingly portrayed as a mute, absent presence. However,
the conventional gender roles associated with the hunting trope
are subtly displaced in the poem. The woman typifies untamed and
inconstant femininity, and unlike the immobile Beloved of Petrarchism, she is at liberty to 'range' and seek new prey, thus taking
on the guise of the male hunter. In contrast, the speaker occupies the
meek, passive, confined position traditionally allocated to women. The
woman takes the dominant role in lovemaking. Once she risked
danger to take bread from the speaker's hand, but outgrows her
dependency unlike, perhaps, the loyal and principled courtier.

    The pain articulated by Wyatt's poem registers on both an erotic
and a political level: thwarted love also stands for a frustrated
desire for power. While the poem eschews the 'jargon' of courtly love
in favour of 'closely reasoned introspection' (Peterson 1967: 102),
it also seems to articulate an inability to offer a creative alternative
to the conventions of the Petrarchan mode and, implicitly, the
restrictions of court (Waller 1993: 113). The speaker's 'gentleness'

suggests his non-aggressive masculinity, and implies too his traditional civility and decorum, which has been abused and exploited by his lover's 'new-fangleness'. Her 'unkindly' faithlessness is typical of her kind, but she remains a 'gentle' woman since her actions are governed by current fashion. The poem bitterly acknowledges that the woman 'is both a wild, uncivil thing and the epitome of a new courtly mode of behaviour whose "newfangled" immorality has superseded the old-fashioned, chivalrous codes of the lover' (Heale 1998: 52). 'They Flee from Me' demonstrates how the traditional conventions of the Petrarchan love lyric are transformed formally and philosophically by the particular circumstances of English court culture.

Even for poets at the outer reaches of the court, Petrarchism constituted the dominant currency in the search for patronage and favour. In Shakespeare's *Sonnets* the persona is variously a pleading lover and a 'socially insecure petitioner searching for an influential patron' (Waller 1993: 223). A number of sonnets present different ways of attacking Petrarchan conventions, however, with the Dark Lady counterposed to Petrarch's Laura:

130
My mistress' eyes are nothing like the sun;
Coral is far more red than her lips' red;
If snow be white, why then her breasts are dun;
If hairs be wires, black wires grow on her head.
I have seen roses damasked, red and white,
But no such roses see I in her cheeks;
And in some perfumes is there more delight
Than in the breath that from my mistress reeks.
I love to hear her speak, yet well I know
That music hath a far more pleasing sound;
I grant I never saw a goddess go;
My mistress, when she walks, treads on the ground.
And yet, by heaven, I think my love as rare
As any she belied with false compare.
                              (Shakespeare 2006: 91)

The poem offers an ironic version of the *blason*, in which the Beloved's individual physical attributes are itemised and praised.

It dwells instead on the mistress's imperfections, demystifying her power and emphasising the lover's disappointment and disillusion. All that is promised or imagined proves false. The sonnet seeks to define and assert what love is by demonstrating what love *is not*, and by highlighting the gap between idealism and experience. In one sense, Sonnet 130 is firmly in the Petrarchan tradition, which has loss, absence, contradiction and the lover's vulnerability at its heart. Even more strikingly than Wyatt's 'They Flee From Me', however, Shakespeare's sonnet also marks a distinct break with the conventions of Petrarchism. Although the poem turns into an equivocal compliment, its ironic treatment of the courtly poem suggests the generic and philosophical limitations of the game of love. The disappointment expressed in Wyatt's poem stems from a sense of private betrayal rather than a loss of faith in courtly values: Sonnet 130 exposes the hollowness of those values and conventions.

Since the notion of a poetic self is largely a product of the sixteenth-century love lyric, where does this leave the 'I' of Shakespeare's sonnet? What alternative means of self-definition is available for the lyric persona? As Waller argues, the dark uncertainties of Shakespeare's sonnets represent both 'the culmination and destruction' of Petrarchism, and 'anticipate the intensification and the demise of the lyric in its characteristic form' (Waller 1993: 223). The 'characteristic' courtly lyric represents an arena in which the gentleman can display his poetic accomplishments; yet in the late sixteenth and early seventeenth centuries, the lyric also offers a stage on which the question of subjectivity – what it means to be an 'I' who writes and is also written about – can be played out.

SPEAKING PLAINLY: DRAMATISING THE SELF

Debates about the purposes, subject matter and forms of lyric are intertwined with wider questions about the nature of poetic language and voice in sixteenth- and seventeenth-century English poetry. Central to these questions is the contest between the so-called plain and eloquent styles that marks lyric practice in the period. The eloquent style was cultivated as a class distinction (Peterson 1967: 6), and was associated with the embellished literary language of court poetry, while the plain style represented a turn towards the vernacular. Both styles were medieval inheritances. The eloquent style derived from ideas of *elecutio*, which involved verbal embellishment and invention, and was also influenced by treatises on rhetoric and learned forms of lyric. The plain style owed its allegiance to proverbial, didactic and 'everyday' types of religious and secular lyric. In practice, these styles often intermingled in early modern lyric. The courtly poem accommodated popular song, giving a demotic flavour to Petrarchan discourse, while the plain style was eminently suited to the high moral purpose of lyric, as proposed by Sidney's *Apology*.

Lyric was centrally involved in the attempts to refine English poetic language (*ibid.*: 40), an enterprise that had to negotiate between these alternative styles. In *The Arte of English Poesie*, Puttenham declared that Wyatt and Henry, Earl of Surrey:

> had tased the sweete and stately measures and stile of the Italian poesie ... they greatly polished our rude and homely manner of vulgar [vernacular] poesie, from that it had bene before.
>
> (Heale 1998: 48)

Although Wyatt and Surrey deployed the same poetic conventions, they offered different brands of lyric. The 'Golden Age' of lyric verse, later venerated by Francis Palgrave in the later nineteenth century, was renowned for its elegance and melodic qualities, epitomised by Surrey's 'Love, That Doth Reign and Live Within my Thought' and 'Alas! So All Things Now Do Hold Their Peace'. This style contrasted with Wyatt's 'rougher' diction and metrical irregularity, which gave the Italian style a vernacular English twist. The Egerton manuscript version of Wyatt's 'They Flee from Me' had its 'rough' metrics later 'tidied' by Tottel when he reprinted it in his *Miscellany*. Although Tottel's collection was 'dedicated to the honor of the Englishe tong, and for the profit of the studious of Englishe eloquence', it contained examples of both the eloquent and vernacular styles. The turn towards the direct and vernacular accorded with the emphasis on masculine vigour in Henry VIII's court. English gradually became the official language of government and diplomacy, rather than Latin and French, and Henry's break from the Church of Rome underpinned this transition.

The business of the court, and of diplomatic missions, demanded a flexible language that could incorporate advice, moral guidance, praise, flattery and manipulation: precisely the range of roles performed by the lyric poet (Heale 1998: 117).

This debate over poetic diction and verse forms attested to wider social and political changes. The ability to produce lyric poetry was still an accomplishment of the gentry, but the gradual move in the seventeenth century away from an elevated poetic style reflected a social transformation. This was due in part to the increasing professionalisation of the writer, and in part to a growing disaffection with the court, which was being challenged by a growing mercantile class, and by a more independent-minded House of Commons. If Elizabethan lyrics exhibit the confidence of an elitist culture, it can be argued that John Donne's secular lyrics 'posit the passing of court as the only significant social and culture centre' (Parfitt 1992: 27). Donne's 'The Anniversarie' appears to articulate a significant aesthetic and ideological shift: 'All Kings, and all their favourites,/ All glory of honours, beauties, wits,/ ... to their destruction draw', while 'Only our love hath no decay' (Donne 1985: 68). There was a brief reassertion of this Elizabethan confidence in the 1630s and early 1640s. The lyrics of poets such as Carew, Suckling and Waller, characterised by their brevity, elegance and cultivated amateurism, are a throwback to the Golden Age. Yet the poetic adornment of the Caroline court needs to be set within the context of impending conflict between Charles I and Parliament. Similarly, the Restoration lyric is often seen to be personified by the libertinism of Rochester, but the monarchy ruled on very different terms after the Civil War. Correspondingly, the poetry associated with court in this period exhibits 'doubt and disbelief' (Parfitt 1992: 48), despite its apparently confident and carefree manner.

In spite of these qualifications, however, the courtly love poem remains the dominant template for lyric, whether its language is eloquent or plain. Donne rehearses Petrarchan conventions, even as he struggles to rewrite them: his poems deal with the frustrations and uncertainties of love, and dwell on the inadequacy of language to express feeling. 'The Canonization' opposes the values of love to the values of the court but, although the lovers appear 'divorced from the wider world' (Parfitt 1992: 24), the power of the court 'is never questioned' (Waller 1993: 234). In the poem, the lovers have withdrawn from the world and, implicitly, from the courtly ideal: love is no longer about seeking favour from an impossibly remote and changeable figure. The speaker abjures public responsibility, and the autonomous pursuit of love will not alter or injure the course of commerce, war or litigation. Yet, so that the couple's love can be 'Canoniz'd', the speaker urges his lover to 'Beg from above/ A patterne of our love'. Whether regal or divine, a higher authority must 'approve' (confirm) whatever the lover is encouraged to 'approve', in the sense of experiencing or attempting. Rather than escaping 'Countries, Townes and Courts', the poem reflects back to the reader the constraints it seeks to evade. This is illustrated by the famous metaphor of 'A Valediction Forbidding Mourning', which portrays the lovers as twin compasses, with the poet circling around a fixed point, ranging freely but always anchored by the firm foot of the other. The conceit represents a mirror of the social world in which the poem operates: autonomy is licensed, and movement is dependent on a fixed, central point. In 'The Good Morrow', the maturity of love is not analogous to pastoral purity and innocence but, by implication, to the sophistication and worldliness of court and city:

> I wonder by my troth, what thou, and I
> Did, till we lov'd? were we not wean'd till then?
> But suck'd on countrey pleasures, childishly?
>> (Donne 1985: 48)

'The Sunne Rising' declares love an independent realm, but this sovereignty is defined throughout in relation to royal power. Love can only be free by matching, rather than ignoring, the authority of the court:

> She'is all States, and all Princes, I,
> Nothing else is.
> Princes doe but play us, compar'd to this,
> All honor's mimique; All wealth alchimie.
>> (ibid.: 54)

The unspoken realisation underlying this confidence is that the intimate space of the bedroom, the centre of the lovers' world, offers only a momentary retreat from the demands of the outside world.

Nonetheless, the linking of creative independence, erotic freedom and privacy in 'The Canonization', where the speaker announces to his lover that 'We'll build in sonnets pretty rooms', presents passion as an alternative to the conventions and constraints of civil society. As Richard Halpern argues, Donne's exploration of these 'rooms', in which one can withdraw from the complexity and seeming 'fragmentation' of the external world, is representative of the modernizing process itself. In 'The Good Morrow', while 'sea-discoverers to new worlds have gone', love 'makes one little roome an every where', and thus renders the increasingly strange and unknowable external world comprehensible to the lovers. The poem revolves not around an opposition between the public and the private, but between 'a dizzying multiplication of worlds on the one hand, and a single, unifying world on the other' (Halpern 1999: 109). The scale and variety of worlds being opened up by exploration and experiment in the early seventeenth century can be reduced to the mutual gaze of the lovers, and enables them to 'possesse one world'. As such, Donne's 'rooms' do not represent a space of lofty disengagement or utopian escape from society: rather, his lyrics are 'a form of historical and social testimony' (*ibid.*: 105) to the often bewildering experience of modernity in the period.

Donne came from a Catholic family, and thus could not hope to attain significant advancement at court. He converted to Anglicanism at the end of the sixteenth century, and in his public career had to demonstrate tact and loyalty to a religious faith and polity that had hitherto been alien to him. His love lyrics mirror this qualified distance from the centre of power, both imitating and demystifying the Petrarchan model. Donne's *Songs and Sonnets* adopts a variety of poetic forms and, in contrast to Elizabethan sequences that concentrate predominantly on the relationship with a particular female figure, the lyrics are populated by a series of shadowy, barely defined women who lack any physical specificity. The self-abasing lover is gone and, as George Parfitt observes, the mistress is replaced by the poet–lover as the main focus of the lyrics. The narrative coherence of a sequence such as Sidney's *Astrophil and Stella* derives from its central figure. In contrast, the coherence of Donne's *Songs and Sonnets* 'is a projection of moods and incidents united only by the poetic personality and style of the writer' (Parfitt 1992: 25).

This changing valuation of lyric is reflected in Donne's poetic forms and language. The stress on wit, vigorous argumentation and persuasion, rather than ornament and embellishment, in Donne's lyrics clearly derives from the plain style. They deploy courtly themes and conventions, but use colloquial and conversational language. Yet this witty, argumentative and often harsh speech also suggests the intimate reflectiveness of the represented voice, drawing attention to the thinking self. This combination of directness and interiority finds two main expressions in the later sixteenth and early seventeenth centuries: in the metaphysical poetry associated particularly with Donne, and in dramatic verse.

Plainer, direct diction that masked philosophical complexity and rhetorical skill made explicit a mode of poetic performance that had always been a central part of the Petrarchan tradition. As Michael Spiller observes: 'The sonnet's lyric voice is a dramatic construct ... the sonnet, from the very beginnings of its long career in the thirteenth century, has offered its readers a variety of fictional positions' (Spiller 1992: 6). This dramatic style evokes the changing moods and emotions of the speaker, and can 'foreground the problems of identity and courtly positioning' in a new fashion (*ibid.*: 119). For example, Sidney introduces stops, starts and inversions in his sonnets in order to create the illusion of the hesitations and reflections of a speaking voice, reminiscent of troubadour poetic song. This is evident in Sonnet 69 from *Astrophil and Stella*:

O joy, too high for my low style to show,
O bliss, fit for a nobler state than me!
Envy, put out thine eyes, lest thou do see
What oceans of delight in me do flow.
My friend, that oft saw through all masks my woe,
Come, come, and let me pour myself on thee:

Gone is the winter of my misery;
My spring appears; O see what here doth grow.
For Stella hath, with words where faith doth shine,
Of her high heart given me the monarchy;
I, I, O I may say, that she is mine.
And though she give but thus conditionly
This realm of bliss, while virtuous course I take,
No kings be crowned but they some covenants make.

(Sidney 1962: 200)

In many respects, the sonnet presents a familiar Petrarchan scenario, offering up a hymn of praise and devotion to an idealised other. It is apparently celebratory, even triumphal, yet its recipient is not clearly defined, and the tone is uneven. The remote, idealised Stella is the subject of the poem, but not the addressee. Is the poem addressed to an intimate confidant, or is it a private reflection? It represents a more qualified profession of love than in Sonnet 68, discussed earlier. The 'realm of bliss' is given 'conditionly', and there is a shift from faith and delight to covenants, commitments, obligations. Transcendent love is bound by temporal contract. Note particularly the difficulty of declaring what the 'I' has sovereignty over. Should we treat 'I, I, O I may say, that she is mine' as a confident declaration, or does it suggest hesitation and anxiety? We saw earlier in Wyatt the uncertainty that besets the courtly lyric, but here it is woven into the structure and rhythm of address. If this poem is read aloud, the heavy caesurae can enable the reader either to stress the speaker's emphatic confidence and conviction, or to draw attention to the interrupted, faltering progress of the statement. The sonnet is full of performatives: it issues pleas and commands to an interlocutor, a reader, or an audience, and attempts to persuade by assuming dramatic form. Yet at the same time the sonnet has a meditative quality, which suggests its psychological depth. Read in this way – the poems may well have been performed originally for a small circle of friends – the sonnet can be seen as the counterpart of dramatic soliloquy.

In Chapter 2 we considered an approach to lyric, particularly associated with New Criticism, that treats it as a drama or dramatic utterance. This harks back to Aristotle, who saw lyric as a mode that punctuates and adorns, but still contributes to, the surrounding drama. Chapter 4 considers the relationship of the Victorian and Modernist dramatic monologue to the non-dramatic lyric, but perhaps the most obvious affinity between drama and lyric comes in the form of soliloquy. John Stuart Mill's 'What is Poetry?' treats soliloquy as the essence of all poetic utterance: 'All poetry is of the nature of soliloquy ... no trace of consciousness that any eyes are upon us must be visible in the work itself.' When this unconsciousness is lost, then so, too, is the quintessential quality of lyric poetry:

> when he [the poet] turns round and addresses himself to another person; when the act of utterance is not itself the end, but a means to an end, – viz. by the feelings he himself expresses, to work upon the feelings, or upon the belief, or the will, of another, – when the expression of his emotions, or of his thoughts tinged by his emotions, is tinged also by that purpose, by that desire of making an impression upon another mind, then it ceases to be poetry, and becomes eloquence.
>
> (Mill 1973: 80)

Mill's clear distinction between rhetoric and expressiveness exemplifies the difference between neoclassical and Romantic conceptions of lyric. Eloquence for Mill equates to rhetorical persuasion, and this has no place in poetry. Genuine poetic expression does not draw attention to itself; it is unconscious of its effects, unaware of an eavesdropper or potential interlocutor. Yet soliloquy is manifestly a dramatic mode of address, however 'unconscious' its performance may appear to be.

In both soliloquy and lyric, there is a tension between presentation and dramatic utterance on the one hand, and 'unconscious' expression on the other. In theatrical terms, this distance between inner and outer can be characterised as the gap between the stage (the poem as an actual, or imagined, performance to an audience), and the page, with its different formal complexities. This blurring between a self that is overheard, and a self that is performed, is keenly apparent in Elizabethan and Jacobean drama.

The soliloquy represents a moment of lyric intensity, lending the appearance of psychological depth that is given dramatic expression. As a formal device, the soliloquy depicts a 'private' mode of expression that abstracts itself from the main action. Yet it addresses an audience and usually performs an important role in the development of the play, for example laying bare the motivations of a character. In addition, as Richard Bradford points out, we can construct an absent addressee and 'background information' from both soliloquy and the isolated non-dramatic lyric (Bradford 1993: 41). While the soliloquy introduces a pause, a moment of reflection and introspection, it is often also a highly rhetorical, powerful utterance that poses questions central to the drama. We might think here of Edmund's speech in *King Lear*, or Macbeth's murderous vision:

> Is this a dagger which I see before me,
> The handle toward my hand? Come, let me clutch thee:
> I have thee not, and yet I see thee still.
> Art thou not, fatal vision, sensible
> To feeling as to sight? or art thou but
> A dagger of the mind, a false creation,
> Proceeding from the heat-oppressèd brain?
> I see thee yet, in form as palpable
> As this which now I draw.
>
> (Shakespeare 1997: II.i. 33–41)

Macbeth is alone with his 'fatal vision', but whether we read the printed text or sit in the audience, we overhear his agony of conscience as he conjures up the dagger. Yet the performatives addressed to the invisible object, the linking of voice, sight, movement and gesture in the speech, and the rhythmic variations mark this out as a stylised internal dialogue. As we saw with Keats's 'This Living Hand' in the previous chapter, the written lyric utterance can stress the here and now, but this directness and authenticity are both produced, and betrayed, by the artfulness of the poem's formal structure and metrical pattern.

Viewed in this way, the dramatic power of lyric derives from elaborate artifice rather than authentic speech. The immediacy and apparent sincerity of the speaking presence is an effect produced by rhetorical skill, complex verse forms, and a fictive suspension of time and space. Yet the strenuous persuasion and 'plain' speaking that mark the metaphysical verse of Donne and others represent a distinct shift in lyric practice. Donne's poetry hinges on the power of address and invocation, and seems to bear out the New Critical contention that each lyric is a 'little drama'. His lyrics are commonly read in terms of dramatic conventions, as the remarks of C. A. Patrides demonstrate: 'We accept that Donne's poems are dramatic, and more specifically dramatic monologues presupposing a listener. Each has in consequence its particular "voice", its distinct narrator; and each, its own "theatrical" language' (Donne 1985: 23). This theatrical language includes the extravagant analogies and extended metaphors or conceits characteristic of the metaphysicals. Conviction and purpose, rather than generic convention or the demands of eloquence, shape what is said. Donne deploys both regular and 'rough' rhythms 'to suggest the nuances of the speaking voice' (Hobsbaum 1996: 40). Scenarios are constructed in which the poet–lover presents compelling arguments to, and urges assent from, an addressee. Donne's lyrics 'ask to be read with the immediacy of a stage performance, with the urgency and authority of the speaking voice and a sense of a multiplicity of an audience which is required to validate and assess their demands' (Waller 1993: 232).

The opening of 'The Canonization' is explicit in its dramatic address: 'For Godsake hold your tongue, and let me love' (Donne 1985: 57). The startling impact of such an utterance is not only sharply different from the polish and decorum of the Elizabethan lyric, it also raises uncertainties about the context and addressee of this statement. Is it directed towards the poet's beloved other, to a figure who thwarts the lover, to one who is unconvinced by his argument or declaration of feeling, or to a single interlocutor who occupies all three roles? Even if Donne's personae constantly strive to monopolise the conversation, a dialogue implicitly takes place. The *Songs and Sonnets* contains a range of voices, presents no consistent poetic self or point of view, and favours contradiction over closure. To an extent, Donne's lyrics suggest the open questions and lack of resolution observed in Macbeth's soliloquy.

We have seen how Donne questions Petrarchism, and does so in urgent speech that invites an audience to judge its claims. While the lyric style favours the strenuous and direct over the ornate and abstract, the situations, ideas and feelings it presents are far from straightforward. The self-dramatisation in Donne stages an 'I' that is more fractured and unstable than in the typical Petrarchan lyric. This is 'court' poetry in a different sense. Lyric becomes a kind of theatre in which the poetic persona tries to advance a case. In the sixteenth century, the courtly lyric put the poetic self on trial in a specific sense: its appeal for recognition and reward was made to a small number of jurors. The dramatic persona in Donne seeks to persuade through wit and conviction, but it addresses a less clearly defined audience. This change in lyric utterance is inextricably linked to changing ways of thinking about, presenting and displaying the self. A modern, self-conscious lyric self emerges in this period, breaking decisively from the anonymous medieval 'I'. This poetic self 'is invested with a keen anxiety about identity, a longing for a stable centre' (Waller 1993: 97). This 'keen anxiety' revolves in part around the location of that 'stable centre'. Lyric continues to be the poetry of display, praise and occasion, but it also increasingly becomes the poetry of meditation and introspection. Thus lyric offers a way of mediating between public and private life, of serving *and* critiquing the interests of power.

SOCIETY AND SECLUSION

Joshua Scodel stresses that the 'personal lyric, conceived as the expression of a highly individualised voice and subjective feeling' is not a major feature of poetry written between the metaphysical period and the late eighteenth century (Scodel 1998: 118). As this book emphasises, the history of lyric in English poetry is not a smooth, linear progression from rhetoric to expression, public to private, performance to meditation. Given the social and political transformations in the British Isles in this period, the turn to more 'public' lyric forms is perhaps unsurprising. The classic, 'greater' ode, drawing on Greek and Roman models and aimed at making 'a rhetorically weighty intervention in public events' (*ibid.*: 119), becomes a central component of lyric practice. Marvell's 'An Horatian Ode upon Cromwell's Return from Ireland' (Marvell 2003: 273–79) acknowledges Horace's political odes in praise of the Emperor Augustus at a time of stability and strength for Rome. In its allusions to Horace and to Lucan's *Pharsalia*, however, Marvell's ode also echoes the Roman poets' ambiguous response to power and justice. The poem is ostensibly epideictic, written to honour a ruler who has brought order, but its praise of the new Puritan order is ambivalent. The praise for the campaign to put down rebellion in Ireland is hedged with equivocation. The ode highlights the nobility of Charles I's bearing when facing execution, an act that confirmed Parliament's 'forcèd power':

> *He* nothing common did or mean
> Upon that memorable scene:
> But with his keener eye
> The axe's edge did try.
>
> (*ibid.*: ll. 57–60)

The courage and honour displayed by Charles is contrasted with Cromwell's triumph:

> What may not then our isle presume,
> While victory his crest does plume!
> What may not others fear,
> If thus he crown each year!
> A Caesar he ere long to Gaul,
> To Italy an Hannibal,
> And to all states not free,
> Shall climactèric be.
>
> (*ibid.*: ll. 97–104)

These stanzas place Cromwell in the pantheon of great military victors, but neither Gaul nor Italy was granted freedom by Caesar and Hannibal. It is thus inferred that the states 'not free' (including, perhaps, England itself) in this moment of historical change can expect invasion and conquest rather than liberation.

Indeed, Cromwell was to invade Scotland only two months after his return from Ireland.

The reworking of the Pindaric Ode in the 1650s, the most prominent exponents of which are Abraham Cowley and John Dryden, is the more popular and sustained development in lyric form, and at the time it was regarded as 'the highest, quintessential' type of lyric (Scodel 1998: 119). Cowley's adaptation of Pindaric panegyrics, which were originally written to celebrate athletic victories in ancient Greece, serve particular occasions – including marriages, funerals, success in warfare – and bestow praise on monarchs, generals, the nobility, scientists and writers. In contrast to the formal regularity of its classical predecessor, the English Pindaric Ode is a relatively free verse form, and is adapted flexibly by poets. Cowley, in particular, is faithful to the spirit of the Pindaric in his ambivalence towards the powerful. Pindar praises his patrons by also cautioning against the dangers of pride and ambition; Cowley's Odes, while generally celebratory, can also function as a vehicle for the expression of indirect criticism of public figures. Cowley was arrested as a Royalist spy by the Puritan regime, and like that of Marvell, his writing expresses carefully qualified support for the new polity. His *Pindaric Odes*, published in 1656, contain political poems that reluctantly concede and acknowledge the Royalist defeat. However, Cowley's ode celebrating the Restoration of the monarchy in 1660 returns to epideictic mode: Cromwell is associated unambiguously with destructive might, while Charles II is elevated to Christ-like status, and the rightful return of the monarchy represents Christ's *'Power Divine'* (Cowley 1905: 420–32). The reworking of the Pindaric mode provides a clear example of how the lyric, which comes to be regarded in most critical accounts as 'timeless' and abstracted from the contexts of its production, has been shaped by, and participates in, the historical moment.

Throughout the seventeenth and eighteenth centuries, however, the 'high' lyric of occasions and commemorations coexists with 'lighter' forms of verse. These include love poems that are often bawdy in tone and content, drinking songs and epigrams. Epigram treats a range of subjects, from compliments, declarations of love and epitaphs to anecdotes and witty remarks. Although the terseness of epigram satisfies the criterion of brevity, its 'plain, and rhetorically low' style is often contrasted to lyric; in *L'Arte Poetica* (1564) Antonio Sebastiano Minturno made clear distinctions between the musical, lyrical quality of the sonnet and the epigram (Fowler 1982: 138). Thus epigram can be situated within the debates about poetic language discussed earlier in this chapter. In practice, poets such as Ben Jonson, Donne and Robert Herrick could move easily between epigrammatic and 'loftier' types of lyric, and Dryden's 'Epigram on Milton' (1688) demonstrates the weightier character of the mode. The eighteenth century is the high point of the witty, satirical epigram. The heroic couplet particularly lends itself to the epigrammatic statement, as many of Alexander Pope's closed couplets demonstrate:

> You beat your pate, and fancy wit will come;
> Knock as you please, there's nobody at home!
> > (Pope 1954: 'Epigram III', 348)

> True ease in writing comes from art, not chance,
> As those move easiest who have learned to dance.
> > (*ibid.*: 'An Essay on Criticism', ll. 361–62; Pope 1993: 29)

Religious poetry moves between the higher and lower forms of lyric in the period. The 'sublime' religious lyric uses the 'high' style of the Pindaric ode to praise the grandeur and boundlessness of God's majesty. The hymn is the other main type of religious lyric, particularly in the non-conformist tradition. It substitutes the elevation of the sublime lyric for 'clear, concise expressions of devotion' (Scodel 1998: 126) that could be sung by a group of worshippers, but as in the ode, the 'I' is communal rather than individual. In his anthology of Augustan lyric verse, Donald Davie has declared the eighteenth century as 'the great age of English hymn-writing' (Davie 1974: 6), and its most notable exponents of the form are Isaac Watts, Charles Wesley and William Cowper. (Chapters 5 and 6 consider eighteenth-century secular and religious lyrics in greater detail.) Elegy, another major lyric form in the seventeenth and eighteenth centuries, draws on Pindaric funerary traditions and operates in both religious and secular contexts. Elegiac poems can take public, commemorative form, express private grief, or mix praise for the deceased with attacks on those still living. Many Civil War poems, such as Marvell's 'An Elegy upon the Death of My Lord Francis Villiers', remember dead Royalists, and 'An Horatian Ode' can be read in part as an elegy for Charles I. In the early seventeenth century, elegies are overtly Christian, even if poems like Milton's 'Lycidas' are heavily indebted to the pastoral elegy of classical antiquity. Dryden's 'To the Memory of Mr Oldham' (1684), however, looks exclusively to classical rather than Christian precedents for consolation. In the eighteenth century, elegy increasingly adopts a secular and personal register, epitomised by Thomas Gray's 'Elegy Written in a Country Churchyard'. The stress in Pope's poetic epitaphs in the 1720s and 1730s is on individual mourning rather than the panegyric.

Alongside the serious, celebratory and ceremonial forms of secular and religious lyric, then, there are new kinds of meditative verse that are influenced by the Pindaric, and that reflect the growing concern with private sentiment demonstrated in elegy. Ben Jonson's 'To Penshurst' famously contrasts country and court, and the pastoralism of poets such as Robert Herrick appears to keep its distance from the turbulence of public affairs. Yet the 'retirement' poem must still define itself against the centre of power, in the same way that Donne's love poetry could not wholly break free from the Petrarchan conventions of court lyric. This qualified sense of 'retirement' is epitomised by Marvell's 'The Garden' (Marvell 2003: 155–59). The poem contrasts the ease and simplicity of country life with the travails of court and city, and the 'busy companies of men':

> How vainly men themselves amaze
> To win the palm, the oak, or bays,
> And their uncessant labours see
> Crowned from some single herb or tree,
> Whose short and narrow vergèd shade
> Does prudently their toils upbraid,
> While all flow'rs and all trees do close
> To weave the garlands of repose.
>
> (*ibid.*: ll. 1–8)

The garden represents imaginative and erotic freedom: 'Society is all but rude,/ To this delicious solitude' (*ibid*.: ll. 15–16), and in such repose the mind 'Withdraws into its happiness' (*ibid*.: l. 42). There remains a degree of ambivalence about this shady retreat, however: the mind can be overshadowed and obscured in the 'vergèd' (deflected) shade.

Poems of withdrawal and seclusion thus still offer oblique political and social comment, but to an extent they also anticipate the turn inward associated with the Romantic lyric. Anne Finch's 'The Introduction' (1689) epitomises this mediation between public and private, expression and restraint. It offers a strenuous defence of women's right to practise poetry in the face of male censure and 'mistaken rules', which leave them 'Debarred from all improvements of the mind'. The woman who 'attempts the pen' is regarded as 'an intruder on the rights of men', and despite her soaring ambition 'The hopes to thrive can ne'er outweigh the fears'. In the face of such opposition, retreat into a narrow social and imaginative space is the only strategy:

> Be cautioned, then, my Muse, and still retired;
> Nor be despised, aiming to be admired;
> Conscious of wants, still with contracted wing,
> To some few friends and to thy sorrows sing.
> For groves of laurel wert thou meant;
> Be dark enough thy shades, and be thou there content.
> (Fullard 1990: 25, ll. 59–64)

Finch's 'A Nocturnal Reverie' (1713), which turns away from the declamatory (and masculinised) qualities of the ode, offers an example of this introspective poetics. The poem celebrates the solitude of the night, a time when 'lonely Philomel, still waking, sings'. This mythic female figure, deprived of voice by brutal male violence yet transformed into a creature capable of rapturous music, becomes the presiding genius of this realm of reverie:

> ... silent musings urge the mind to seek
> Something, too high for syllables to speak;
> Till the free soul to a composedness charmed,

Finding the elements of rage disarmed,
O'er all below a solemn quiet grown,
Joys in the inferior world, and thinks it like her own:
In such a night let me abroad remain,
Till morning breaks, and all's confused again;
Our cares, our toils, our clamours are renewed,
Or pleasures, seldom reached, again pursued.

(*ibid.*: 237; ll. 41–50)

Finch associates lyric with solitude, intensity of thought and feeling: it constitutes an imaginative act elevated above the 'toils' and 'clamours' of ordinary life. The lyric mode is posited as a distinct, private and, in Finch's terms, *gendered* sphere. As Scodel points out, '[t]he gender struggles often addressed in Pindaric odes are central to the period's lyrics of love and friendship' (Scodel 1998: 126). As we see from these different writing contexts of Marvell and Finch, lyric practice is often not an escape from, but a complex response to, an inhospitable ideological climate.

THE ODE AND EXPRESSIVE THEORY

From the late seventeenth century onwards, debates about the lyric often revolved around the nature and purpose of the ode, with the Pindaric 'greater ode' considered the finest refinement of the lyric form. Yet literary history often treats the eighteenth century as a barren period for the lyric, a decline reversed only by the radical transformations in poetic practice wrought by Romanticism. Douglas Lane Patey summarises the two opposing views and valuations of lyric in the eighteenth century. On the one hand, the lyric is seen to have a reached a high point of achievement, while on the other hand, poetry – with lyric as its 'purest' example – is treated as an outmoded or trivial form, marked by its incapacity to emulate the classical forerunners and superseded by 'more advanced, "philosophical" uses of mind' (Patey 1993: 587). John Aikin, in his *Essays on Song-Writing* (1772), rejects the commonly held view that 'the moderns fall short of the antients' in lyric poetry, and cites as evidence how 'the graver and sublimer strains of the Lyric muse are exemplified in the modern Ode, a species of composition which admits of the boldest flights of poetical enthusiasm, and the wildest creations of the imagination' (Bergstrom 2002: 3). In *Sketches of a History of Literature* (1794), Richard Alves concludes his discussion of recent lyric poets by declaring that 'no species of poetry is more worthy of notice, and, in no age whatsoever, was lyric poetry cultivated to more advantage' (Patey 1993: 589).

This picture of a golden age is strongly challenged by others, however: lyric is often perceived as a minor literary form, and there is deep suspicion about the contrived expression of feelings in love poems and elegies. Amatory and elegiac verse, sonnets and epigrams are dismissed by Rapin in his *Reflections on Aristotle's Treatise of Poesie* (1694) as 'the meer productions of Imagination', while Temple, in 'Of Poetry' (1690) argues that those who cannot write successful heroic poetry must be satisfied with 'the Scraps, with Songs and Sonnets, with Odes and Elegies' (Abrams 1953: 85). In his 1756 study of Pope, Joseph Warton portrays the modern ode as a poor imitation of its ancient predecessor: 'The moderns have, perhaps, practised no species of poetry with so little success, and with such indisputable inferiority to the ancients, as the ODE' (Patey 1993: 588). As the next chapter argues, the Romantic period later privileges the ode as a poetic form.

Lyric undergoes a more fundamental attack in the eighteenth century from philosophers in France and Germany. In his *Lettres persanes* (1721), Montesquieu condemns poetry for shackling and loading down reason with ornament, reserving his special contempt for the 'melodious nonsense' of lyric poets. Voltaire, in his *Philosophical Dictionary* (1771), insists that the ode has little meaning for the modern world, and its antiquity as a literary form marks its weakness rather than its strength. Hegel's *Aesthetic* goes much further, arguing that poetry could no longer serve the needs of cultural progress (Patey 1993: 589–91). Thus the lyric mode, in particular, is regarded by many as an anachronistic form that lacks the profundity to speak about modernity.

The apparent collapse in the fortunes of the lyric is challenged by the development of expressive theory in later eighteenth century aesthetics that has been traced by M. H. Abrams. This theory places the author at its centre; the lyric form is intimately connected to the poet's state of mind, and any moral or pleasurable effect is merely 'a fortunate by-product of the author's spontaneous expression of feeling' (Abrams 1953: 89). True poetry involves rapture and intense emotion. William Jones's 'Essay on the Arts Called Imitative' (1772) proposes lyric as a prototype for poetry as a whole, partly on the basis of his Orientalist conclusions about 'primitive' Persian, Arabic and Indian poetry that he had translated. He rejects Aristotle's view that poetry is imitation, and defines 'original and native poetry' as the 'language of the violent passions' (*ibid*.: 87). In Jones's account, lyric does not deal in mimesis, unlike narrative and dramatic forms, which imitate the external world through plot and characterisation. Jones's conclusion is shared by J. G. Sulzer, who published his encyclopedia of aesthetics in four volumes between 1771 and 1774. Sulzer identifies lyric as the primordial form, the epitome, of poetry, with the ode as its purest expression: 'the odes constitute the highest poetic kind ... The fashion in which the odist in each instance utters his thoughts and his feelings has more of the poetic in it, than ... [that] of the epic poet, or any other poet' (*ibid*.: 89). The expression of feeling is deemed to be as worthy of the ode as praise of public figures, or comment on political and social matters. Lyric should not, in Joseph Warton's words, be 'minutely historical' (Patey 1993: 600); lyric poetry typifies solitude and retirement, and becomes 'the favoured vehicle for a new vision of selfhood not as informed or constituted by social role' (*ibid*.: 601). As Norman MacLean has noted, this shift of emphasis, from the public or epideictic nature of the ode to the inner sublimity of the poetic imagination, questions the categorical distinctions between 'greater' and 'lesser' forms of lyric proposed in classical and neoclassical theories (MacLean 1952: 459).

In 1797, Anna Laetitia Barbauld schematises this inward turn by dividing poetry into two classes. The external world can be dealt with more effectively by epic, didactic and dramatic verse, while 'pure poetry, or Poetry in the abstract', charts an internal realm:

> It is conversant with an imaginary world, peopled with beings of its own creation. It deals in splendid imagery, bold fiction, and allegorical

personages. It is necessarily obscure to a certain degree; because [it has] to do chiefly with ideas generated within the mind ... All that is properly *Lyric Poetry* is of this kind.

(Patey 1993: 594)

This abstraction or withdrawal, precisely the quality that brings into question the cultural value of lyric poetry for many theorists in the eighteenth century, will often be seen as the signal strength or weakness of lyric over the next two centuries. Although Barbauld is writing in the early Romantic period, her definition of lyric is shaped by a dispute stretching across the eighteenth century. As Carson Bergstrom has demonstrated, in the eighteenth century the lyric genre expresses a new perception and understanding of the natural world associated with experimental science (Bergstrom 2002: 20), and there is an increasing emphasis on defining the character of the lyric experience. Romanticism does not have to happen before the lyric can be theorised in terms of harmony, elevated feeling, heightened expression and an intensified relationship to nature. As Patey observes: 'We should recognize the paradoxical valuation of lyric not as a "preromantic" strain in an otherwise classic eighteenth century, but rather as an instability at the heart of the Augustan literary enterprise itself' (Patey 1993: 595). As we have seen, that paradoxical valuation of lyric is, in turn, shaped by debates in the preceding two centuries.

The competing definitions of lyric in the eighteenth century rehearse the recurrent tensions in attempts to define the properties and value of lyric: it could be dismissed or embraced as light and 'emotional', as serious and intellectual, and as a mode of expression that engaged with, or retreated from, the 'outer' world. Equally, the clear distinctions between epic and lyric, the narrative and the expressive – so prominent in the nineteenth century – have already been drawn. Accounts of the development of lyric have tended to see Romanticism as marking a decisive break with the lyric practice of previous periods. Yet, as this survey of poetic practice and critical debate across three centuries suggests, some of the assumptions underpinning the modern idea of lyric are already visible well before Romanticism arrives.

4

'I WANDERED LONELY'
ROMANTIC AND POST-ROMANTIC LYRIC

At the end of the previous chapter, we saw that the Romantic lyric constituted an evolution rather than a revolution in poetics. As this chapter will demonstrate, the attempt in modern lyric to construct an inward-looking poetic self who is 'overheard' remains crucially dependent on the structure of address. Romantic and post-Romantic lyric still involve both introspection and display, the personal and the public, escapism and 'serious' purpose. The continued reliance on dramatic or performative modes of address over the past two centuries will be traced in exemplary Romantic lyrics and odes, in the prominence of the dramatic monologue and meditative poem from the Victorian and Modernist periods to the present day, and in the 'performance' of the self in contemporary poetry.

Given these important qualifications, it is nonetheless the case that by the later eighteenth century, poetic theory tended to regard lyric as 'the songlike personal expression, the feeling centred in the image' (Wimsatt and Brooks 1965: 433). As Alistair Fowler has observed, almost every genre became lyric in the nineteenth century (Fowler 1982: 206). This is accompanied by the collapsing of various related poetic forms into the general term 'lyric'. According to Paul de Man, 'it would be impossible to speak relevantly about modern literature without giving a prominent place to lyric poetry'. Indeed, for many critics, 'the question of modernity in the lyric is considered as the best means of access to a discussion of literary modernity in general' (de Man 1983: 169). Thus the predominant late modern association of lyric with sincerity, intimacy and the direct expression of feeling becomes all-encompassing in the study of literature. For de Man, however, lyric poetry in the nineteenth and twentieth centuries questions rather than confirms that centrality of the 'I': modern lyric plays out a 'crisis of self and representation' (*ibid.*: 182). A central feature of modern lyric, the autonomous, coherent lyric self becomes the site of its greatest uncertainty. This 'crisis' will now be traced through an examination of the range of voices and personae, and the complex versions of both the writing and the textual self, in Romantic and post-Romantic lyric.

THE ROMANTIC LYRIC

M. H. Abrams has traced the way in which lyric becomes the 'paradigm for poetic theory' in the Romantic period, and its major poetry and criticism 'circles out from the poet as centre' (Abrams 1953: 99). There is a 'tendency to convert the lyric "I" from what Coleridge called the "I-representative" to the poet in his "proper" person' (*ibid.*: 98). Wordsworth's declaration that 'Poetry is the spontaneous overflow of powerful feelings' (Wordsworth 1992: 62) epitomises this elevation of the poet, who becomes synonymous with the lyric 'I'. This model is not universally endorsed by Romantic poets, however. In his speculations on the 'poetical Character', Keats attacked 'the Wordsworthian or egotistical sublime', and defined lyric subjectivity in impersonal terms:

> it is not itself – it has no self – it is every thing and nothing – It has no character – it enjoys light and shade; it lives in gusto, be it foul or fair, high or low, rich or poor, mean or elevated – It has as much delight in conceiving an Iago as an Imogen.
>
> (Keats, letter to Richard Woodhouse, 27 October 1818;
> Gittings 1985: 157)

Keats's emphasis is on the process of writing, rather than 'personality': the poet has no 'identity', and thus the lyric 'I' manifests itself only as a product of textuality. The disappearance of the poet in the act of composition anticipates T. S. Eliot's notion of artistic impersonality almost 100 years later. The range of 'ironizing and critical techniques' (McGann 1998: 250) in Byron's poetry, allied to his use of longer poetic forms with strong narrative and dramatic emphases, also represents an antidote to notions of sincerity, intimacy and self-revelation in Romantic poetry. It can thus be argued that the Romantic lyric is, in significant part, a retrospective construction.

Wordsworth's poetics of personality has nonetheless proved a dominant influence on subsequent understandings of lyric. One of his best known poems, 'I wandered lonely as a cloud' (1804, 1807), illustrates the way in which the figure of the poet is placed centre stage in Romantic lyric:

> I wandered lonely as a cloud
> That floats on high o'er vales and hills,
> When all at once I saw a crowd,
> A host, of golden daffodils;
> Beside the lake, beneath the trees,
> Fluttering and dancing in the breeze.
> Continuous as the stars that shine
> And twinkle on the milky way,
> They stretched in never-ending line
> Along the margin of a bay:
> Ten thousand saw I at a glance,
> Tossing their heads in sprightly dance.
> The waves beside them danced; but they
> Out-did the sparkling waves in glee:
> A poet could not but be gay,
> In such a jocund company:
> I gazed – and gazed – but little thought
> What wealth the show to me had brought:
> For oft, when on my couch I lie
> In vacant or in pensive mood,
> They flash upon that inward eye

Which is the bliss of solitude;
And then my heart with pleasure fills,
And dances with the daffodils.

(Wordsworth 1986: 303–4)

The poem elevates the 'I' literally and metaphorically: the poet 'floats on high', lost in thought before suddenly gazing down on the daffodils. The 'I' walks in the 'bliss of solitude', and the scene is enjoyed privately. The vivid, rhapsodic experience of witnessing the daffodils momentarily releases the sensitive self from the bounds of time and space: in a 'flash' of recollection, the speaker can be transported back to treasure this 'wealth' once more. 'I wandered lonely' works hard to place us in the here and now, to encourage us to share in the wonder and beauty of the scene. Yet the 'original' experience has gone: this lyric moment is a product of reflection rather than spontaneity. Theatrical terminology – 'dancing', 'show', 'company' – is deployed to evoke the natural display of the flowers, but it is the 'inward eye' of the solitary observer that orchestrates the spectacle. This chance encounter is staged by the imagination, and the outer world is shaped by an inner landscape.

The poem suggests that the memory arises complete and unprompted from the 'vacant' or 'pensive' mood, but this is a work of active imagination. The journal entry of his sister Dorothy for 15 April 1802 suggests the origins of this revelatory personal moment for Wordsworth:

I never saw daffodils so beautiful they grew among the mossy stones about & about them, some rested their heads upon these stones as on a pillow for weariness & the rest tossed & reeled & danced & seemed as if they verily laughed with the wind that blew upon them over the lake, they looked so gay ever glancing ever changing.

(Dorothy Wordsworth 1991: 85)

The re-imagining of the scene, via the words of the other (unidentified) witness, clearly qualifies the individuality and directness of the feelings expressed in the poem. In his Preface to *Lyrical Ballads* (1802, 1805), Wordsworth acknowledges the combination of simplicity and complexity, directness and long reflection that constitutes the lyric moment celebrated in 'I Wandered Lonely'. While 'all good poetry is the spontaneous overflow of powerful feelings', poems 'to which any value can be attached, were never produced on any variety of subjects but by a man who, being possessed of more than usual organic sensibility, had also thought long and deeply' (Wordsworth 1992: 62). Poetry therefore 'takes its origin from emotion recollected in tranquillity' (*ibid.*: 82). In poems such as 'Nutting', the Lucy sequence, and throughout *The Prelude*, stories are 'established precisely by the gap between the "now" of the poem's composition and the "then" of the experience it records' (Lindley 1985: 71). Although Wordsworth's lyric highlights personal feeling and raw experience, the textual persona is fashioned through the *simulation* of spontaneity and authenticity. Thus we might argue that it is as indebted to display and rhetorical persuasion as the most ostentatious courtly poem from the sixteenth century.

The intense communion with a specific natural scene in 'I wandered lonely' represents in miniature the poetic form described by M. H. Abrams as the 'greater Romantic lyric'. The 'greater' lyric presents

> a determinate speaker in a particularized, and usually, a localized, outdoor setting, whom we overhear as he carries on, in a fluent vernacular which rises easily to a more formal speech, a sustained colloquy, sometimes with himself or with the outer scene, but more frequently with a silent human auditor, present or absent.
>
> (Abrams 1970: 527–28)

This form of lyric superseded what neoclassical critics termed the elevated, Pindaric 'greater ode', yet the greater lyric was a direct descendant of the neoclassical 'local' poem, which described, and also 'interpreted', a geographical location. The local poem could be used for morally instructive purposes by focusing on topographical features that suggested a correspondence between the natural and divine world. This didactic element is maintained in the greater lyric, as is the emphasis on local detail. A number of the most notable Romantic place poems, such as Wordsworth's 'Lines Written a Few Miles above Tintern Abbey' (13 July 1798),

Coleridge's 'The Eolian Harp, Composed at Clevedon, Somersetshire' and 'This Lime-Tree Bower My Prison' (June 1797), and Shelley's 'Stanzas Written in Dejection – December 1818, near Naples' are precisely placed and dated (Abrams 1970: 534). Although this specificity dispels some of the mythology surrounding the ethereal, context-free Romantic lyric, Abrams identifies a 'wide disparity' between the greater lyric and its predecessors. Over the course of the eighteenth century, the local poem had gradually moved inward, concentrating on the experience of the speaker rather than on scenic detail, and in 'the fully developed Romantic lyric', topographical description becomes subordinate to a meditation that is 'sustained, continuous, and highly serious' (*ibid*.: 552).

The serious intent of the greater lyric can be seen in the ascent of the Alps or Snowdon in *The Prelude*, in Shelley's 'Mont Blanc', or in the rapturous elevation of the ode. This notion of poetry as a 'region to wander in' (Keats, letter to Benjamin Bailey, 8 October 1817; Gittings 1985: 27) echoes the sublime magnitude and interiority that Anna Laetitia Barbauld associated with lyric at the end of the eighteenth century. The ambition of Romantic lyric is epitomised by Mme de Stael's remark in 1813: to appreciate 'the true grandeur of lyric poetry, one must wander in thought into the ethereal regions ... and regard the whole universe as a symbol of emotions of the soul' (Abrams 1953: 91). Yet the meditative nature of the greater lyric, which involves a sensitive self whose 'inward eye' transforms the external landscape, is perhaps better exemplified by Wordsworth's 'Tintern Abbey'. As in 'I Wandered Lonely', the immediacy of experience gives way to reflection and a sense of loss. The poet discerns the difference between the present landscape and the 'wild secluded scene' perceived 'five summers' ago (Wordsworth 1992: 207, ll. 1–5), and cannot paint 'What then I was'. The intense, direct encounter with nature was an 'appetite' that 'had no need of a remoter charm,/ By thought supplied, nor any interest/ Unborrowed from the eye' (*ibid*.: 211, ll. 81–84). The 'aching joys' and 'dizzy raptures' of 'thoughtless youth' have passed, to be replaced by the hope of 'sober pleasures' and a time when memory becomes 'a dwelling-place/ For all sweet sounds and harmonies' (*ibid*.: 214, ll. 142–43). *The Prelude* follows a similar pattern of revisitation. In two episodes from

Book 1, nature initially leads and instructs, before imaginative escape gives way to emptiness and the 'Growth of a Poet's Mind' is temporarily arrested. In an 'act of stealth/ And troubled pleasure', the speaker steals a boat on Ullswater. The horizon stretches ahead, but the sense of freedom and ambition turns into foreboding: 'o'er my thoughts/ There was a darkness, call it solitude/ Or blank desertion' (Wordsworth 1986: 385, ll. 420–22). The speaker recalls skating on Eskdale as 'a time of rapture', yet the clarity of memory and vividness of sensory experience gives way to melancholy: the 'solitary cliffs' stretch behind in 'solemn train', and the speaker drifts into 'dreamless sleep' (387, ll. 484–89). In each case, the gap between past and present, and between experience and writing, is apparent. The Romantic lyric 'interlude' involves the negotiation of two distinct kinds of feeling – the spontaneous and naïve, and the reflexive and internalised (McGann 1998: 251) – and is primarily about withdrawal and loss, rather than ecstasy or plenitude.

Many Romantic poems present a speaker who appears remote from the commotion of the social world, but the intensity and immediacy of the 'spot of time' is enjoyed and made sensible only retrospectively, when the direct stimulus of nature is absent. The lyric moment takes place in a present moment, where poetic meditation must compete with the noise of modernity, all that is not golden and dancing. In 'Tintern Abbey', the recollection of nature's 'forms of beauty' are a solace 'in lonely rooms, and mid the din/ Of towns and cities' (Wordsworth 1992: 208, ll. 23–27). At the end of the nineteenth century, Yeats's 'The Lake Isle of Innisfree' derives similar retrospective comfort from natural solitude while on the 'roadway' and 'pavements grey' (Yeats 1982: 44). While there is a sense of loss in such poems, nature remains a comforting resource. John Clare's poetry provides a striking contrast in its use of nature; his work shows the effects on a lyric 'I' who is not free to wander lonely, and whose relation to the rural environment is characterised by estrangement and disruption rather than emotional attachment and celebration. The speaker of 'I am' is far from secure in solitude: 'I am – yet what I am, none cares or knows;/ My friends forsake me like a memory lost.' Any communion with the landscape is achievable only in death:

I long for scenes where man hath never trod
A place where woman never smiled or wept
There to abide with my Creator God,
And sleep as I in childhood sweetly slept,
Untroubling and untroubled where I lie
The grass below, above, the vaulted sky.

(Clare 1967: 195)

Clare's later 'asylum' lyrics are written in the shadow of psychological breakdown, but the isolation and rootlessness of his poetry are equally shaped by a history of land enclosures and the disintegration of rural communities in the late eighteenth and early nineteenth centuries. Whereas Wordsworth's lyric implies a retreat from the present, Clare's poem represents a complicated engagement with its historical moment.

In other ways, too, the 'greater' lyric is far from timeless and abstracted: dialogue and persuasion are central to many of the most renowned Romantic lyrics. In 'Tintern Abbey' we see landscape through the eye of a poet–speaker whose 'vivid "presence"' is purely fictive, and the text 'works to situate the reader within the speaker' (Easthope 1983: 128–29). Even in its vivid account of the present moment, the poem is somewhere else, as the speaker drifts between past, present and future. Coleridge's 'conversation' poems also involve explicit structures of address, deploying 'the dramatic monologue's vocatives of direct address to a person' rather than formal apostrophes (Shaw1997: 304). The power accorded to spontaneous speech is central to Coleridge's poetry, a point underscored in *Table Talk* (1835), a collection of fragments of his conversations compiled by his nephew Henry Nelson Coleridge. Contemporaneous accounts recall the impact of his words in an age without the means to record speech mechanically: 'I can give no idea of the beauty and sublimity of his conversation. It resembles the sublimity of song; I left him at night so thoroughly magnetized, that I could not for two or three days afterwards reflect enough to put anything down on paper' (cited by Perry 2002: 106–07).

More strictly, perhaps, poems such as 'This Lime-Tree Bower', 'The Eolian Harp' and 'Frost at Midnight' can be treated as dramatised lyrics, as the persona is not readily separable from the individualised, reflective voice of the poet. This is a characteristic feature of Robert Browning's dramatic lyric that will be examined in more detail shortly. Most conversations involve at least two people, and require an act of listening. In the Conversation poems, listeners barely feature at times, but the poems nonetheless depend upon an interlocutor, someone who will hear or receive the poem, even if the response of that listener is uncertain. 'Frost at Midnight' allows us to eavesdrop on an overheard, meditative speaker, but the night is 'so calm, that it disturbs/ And vexes meditation with its strange/ And extreme silentness' (Coleridge 2004: 120, ll. 8–10). The speaker is an 'unquiet thing', longing to break the silence and teach his sleeping son about 'The lovely shapes and sounds intelligible' that he will hear in the future (*ibid.*: 121, ll. 63–64). 'This Lime-Tree Bower' begins in solitude and isolation, but is about companionship and contact: the incapacitated speaker 'joins' the excursion by conducting an imaginary conversation with his friends. 'The Eolian Harp' opens by naming another – the poet's wife, Sara – while 'Tintern Abbey' identifies its ostensible addressee only after 120 lines, and even then it is as 'sister' rather than as 'Dorothy'. If the poet in 'Tintern Abbey' is communing with anyone or anything, it is the natural world, whose 'sweet inland murmur' generates 'Thoughts of more deep seclusion'. Wordsworth's greater lyrics are predominantly conversations with the poetic self, and are closer in spirit than Coleridge to Shelley's idea of the nightingale poet composing in darkness and solitude.

Yet the title of Wordsworth's and Coleridge's *Lyrical Ballads* (1798) juxtaposes the private, introspective lyric mode with the ballad, a form traditionally associated with folk culture, oral narrative and action. The ballad form is typically impersonal, avoids ornamentation, and concentrates on telling a story rather than dwelling on personal feelings. The Preface celebrates living, 'ordinary' speech as the language of lyric through poems that relate events and situations from 'common life' in 'a selection of language really used by men'. The poems focus on the condition of 'rustic' life, where 'the essential passions of the heart find a better soil in which they can attain their maturity, are less under restraint, and speak a plainer and more emphatic language.' This 'plainer' speech recalls debates over the plain and eloquent styles in the seventeenth century, and also the progressive rejection of oratory and rhetoric in modern theories of lyric. The 'high' or serious intent of the lyric, then, is expressed through a poetic language of clarity and simplicity that reflects 'the beautiful and permanent forms of nature' (Wordsworth 1992: 59–60). Wordsworth's 'Simon Lee' and 'We Are Seven', and Coleridge's 'The Rime of the Ancient Mariner', attempt to replicate this simplicity by adopting the narrative directness, and metrical patterns, of ballad. Yet Richard Bradford has termed *Lyrical Ballads* a 'sociocultural confidence trick', since it is an elevated, remote 'I' who gives 'authentic' voice to the 'illiterate, uncultured denizens' of the rural landscape in Wordsworth's poems (Bradford 1993: 99). It is the meditative tourist in 'Tintern Abbey', rather than the marginal figures in 'The Thorn' or 'The Idiot Boy' (akin to Clare's lyric 'I'), who speaks the 'essential passions of the heart'.

The narrative drive associated with the ballad competes constantly with lyric suspension in Wordsworth and Coleridge. To put it simply, in lyric the reader accepts the suspension of time; in narrative the reader demands progress and action. Tilottama Rajan has noted the tendency of modern critics to privilege the 'lonely' Wordsworthian lyric to the exclusion of narrative in *The Prelude*, which misreads how the poetic self is constructed through the poem. The 'Boy of Winander' episode in Book V (ll. 389–413) demonstrates that the poem is a developmental, if discontinuous, story (Rajan 1985: 76). These lines were published separately and could be read as a free-standing lyric poem, the Aristotelian 'mini-drama', discussed in Chapter 2. This self-contained poem appears to celebrate a visionary moment of communion with the natural world, a process that arrests time:

> And when it chanced
> That pauses of deep silence mocked his skill,
> Then sometimes, in that silence, while he hung
> Listening, a gentle shock of mild surprise
> Has carried far into his heart the voice
> Of mountain torrents; or the visible scene

> Would enter unawares into his mind
> With all its solemn imagery, its rocks,
> Its woods, and that uncertain Heaven, received
> Into the bosom of the steady lake.
>   (Wordsworth 1986: 444, ll. 404–13).

This lyric fragment is part of a longer narrative that surrounds it, however: in 'the mind's clear eye' the boy merely 'slumbers' in the present, but in fact he died before he was ten years old. The isolated episode is thus opened to the passage of time, and contributes to the poem's 'epic' momentum. Bradford notes similar tensions in Coleridge's use of the ballad form. In 'The Rime of the Ancient Mariner' and 'Kubla Khan', the narrative impetus stalls, frozen by moments of vision or intense perceptual experience. The poems consist of a series of consecutive events that are not taken to their conclusion, and these points of suspension represent a shift away from narrative towards 'immediacy, in which the primary structural determinant is the mental and linguistic resources of the speaker rather than the objective, consecutive nature of the events – the most familiar manifestation of this being the Romantic Ode' (Bradford 1993: 106).

Philip Cox argues that Abrams's description of the greater lyric is too neatly linear, and subtly effaces the rhetorical and discursive dimensions of earlier lyric practice that remain prominent within and beyond the Romantic period (Cox 1996: 55). This can be seen in the place-poem and in the ode, which demonstrates a continuity with the eighteenth century 'Greater' ode as a 'self-reflexive demonstration of the poet's rhetorical authority' (Creaser 1998: 240) In contrast to the classical ode, however, the Romantic ode is concerned primarily with the one who praises, rather than the one who is praised. It attempts to capture a moment in which the poetic self is transformed, elevated beyond the realm of everyday experience. The speaker exalts, and yearns to be united with, a transcendent presence or force, and the apostrophic appeal to an abstract or remote other is presented as the expression of involuntary, heightened feeling. Pierre Fontanier characterises apostrophe in 1830 as a Wordsworthian 'overflow' of emotion: 'But what can give rise to apostrophe? It can only be feeling, and only the feeling stirred up within the heart until it breaks out and spreads itself about on the outside, as if acting on its own … [as if it were] the spontaneous impulse of a powerfully moved soul!' (Fontanier 1968: 372). Yet the Romantic ode is a vehicle for the poetic voice to establish its credentials rather than an expression of private rapture. As Jonathan Culler observes, the poet invokes the elements, seasons, inanimate objects, creatures or mountains in order to harness or be subsumed by the force of this otherness (Culler 1981: 142).

The declamatory, rhetorical style of Shelley's 'Ode to the West Wind' exemplifies this extravagant ambition:

> Make me thy lyre, even as the forest is:
> What if my leaves are falling like its own!
> The tumult of thy mighty harmonies
> Will take from both a deep, autumnal tone,
> Sweet though in sadness. Be thou, Spirit fierce,
> My spirit! Be thou me, impetuous one!
> Drive my dead thoughts over the universe
> Like withered leaves to quicken a new birth!
> (Shelley 2002: 298–301, ll. 57–64)

'To a Skylark' also strives to be carried away by the 'divine' song of the 'blithe Spirit' it addresses:

> Better than all measures
> Of delightful sound—
> Better than all the treasures
> That in books are found—
> Thy skill to poet were, thou Scorner of the ground!
> (*ibid.*: 304–07, ll. 96–100)

The poet remains earthbound, however, vainly seeking the 'harmonious madness' that such identification would bring. Keats's 'Ode to a Nightingale' (Keats 1977: 346–48) also fails to provide a satisfactory lyric experience, as the speaker is not 'transported' any more than in Shelley's poems (Chase 1985: 212–13). The speaker longs to be submerged in the 'ecstasy' of the bird's song, to 'Fade far away, dissolve, and quite forget/ What thou among the leaves hast never known' (Keats 1977: 346–48, ll. 21–22). The poet can approach the 'light-wingèd' freedom of the 'immortal Bird' only in death or narcotic oblivion. Like Wordsworth's daffodils, the nightingale's fading 'anthem' is a reminder of what the 'I' cannot fully possess. The speaker is left in isolation and uncertainty: 'Was it a vision, or a waking dream?/ Fled is that music – Do I wake or sleep?' (*ibid.*: ll. 79–80). These apostrophes fail to reach their remote addressee, and the 'drama' or 'occasion' of each poem lies in its explicit reflection on that creative failure. Therefore the Romantic apostrophe makes apparent that the poem 'is an event of language rather than a description or narrative of experience' (Furniss and Bath 1996: 128).

The different forms of Romantic lyric discussed in this section might be grouped together under Robert Langbaum's umbrella term, the 'poem of experience'. This poem 'is both subjective and objective. The poet talks about himself by talking about an object; and he talks about an object by talking about himself. Nor does he address either himself or the object, but both together' (Langbaum 1957: 47). This is typified by Shelley's 'Mont Blanc' or the journey through the Alps in the *Prelude*. It constitutes a blurring of the inner and outer worlds: the self is projected onto external nature, which in turn becomes a mirror that reflects back an image of the self. The poetry of experience is dialogical and dramatic, a new genre that 'abolishes the distinction between subjective and objective poetry and between the lyrical and dramatic or narrative genres' (*ibid.*). The greater lyric, the 'conversation' poem and the ode thus anticipate the Victorian turn to dramatic lyric and dramatic monologue. While standard accounts of modern lyric emphasise its progressive retreat from the world, it can be argued that, in fact, lyric in the nineteenth century becomes increasingly anxious to speak to others.

THROUGH ANOTHER'S LIPS: THE DRAMATIC MONOLOGUE AND DRAMATIC LYRIC

Victorian lyric is shaped not only by the tension between narrative progress and lyric suspension, but also by a tension between an overheard and a conversational speaker. Victorian poets inherited the Romantic assumption that the lyric voice was 'autonomous, self-conscious, atemporal' (Slinn 1999: 309), and Mill's rejection of the didactic, rhetorical aspects of poetic language encouraged a consensus in the period that poetry 'was immediate, passionate, imaginative, lyric' (Latane 1999: 395). Yet from the 1830s and 1840s onwards, 'the cultural value of the lyrical voice was in trouble' (Slinn 1999: 309). This was in part due to the predominance of epic and narrative forms in the period, but many poets and commentators also questioned the conventional poetics of lyricism. John Keble argued that the lyric is prey to transitory moods and artificial passions that are too short and fickle. In marked contrast to aesthetic theory in the late eighteenth and early nineteenth centuries, Keble viewed the drama and epic as the primary expressive genres, as in these the poet articulates 'his own thoughts through another's lips' (Abrams 1953: 99). This suggests the dramatic monologue rather than Mill's 'overheard' song, and many Victorian lyric poems are a blend of passionate persuasion, dramatisation and meditation. The questioning of the lyric 'I' is also shaped by a wider philosophical shift in the wake of Hegel's *The Phenomenology of Mind* (1807), which argues that the self is not an autonomous or pre-given category, but is rather constituted through its relation to others. Thus Victorian lyric poetry is less a vehicle for 'private expressiveness' than a 'point where self and world are constructed' (Slinn 1999: 310).

Warwick Slinn argues that dramatic monologue enables Victorian poets to portray extreme feelings or abnormal states of consciousness, and to question the notion of a stable, unified self by highlighting the dialogical nature of language: 'By choosing aberrant or excessive speakers, they kept poetry as a genre for passion, though no longer in the discredited terms of Romantic lyricism: they encouraged the reader to become an active participant and to contemplate the political as well as the psychological significance of the passion indulged' (*ibid.*: 314). Poets such as Elizabeth Barrett Browning and Augusta Webster use the dramatic monologue to give a voice to the voiceless or marginalised. Webster uses mirror images in poems such as 'By the Looking Glass' (1866), 'A Castaway', and 'Circe' (1870), to explore the disconnection between what the protagonist feels and the role or persona imposed upon her by Victorian society. Barrett Browning's 'The Runaway Slave at Pilgrim's Point' (1848) was written at the request of friends involved in the anti-slavery movement in America, and it was displayed at the Boston National Anti-Slavery Bazaar. The poem's directness and rhetorical challenge to the reader is a striking contrast to the overheard lyric. The assertive female speaker is a textual 'I' that does not muse in solitude:

> XXXII
> I am not mad: I am black!
> I see you staring in my face—
> I know you staring shrinking back!
> Ye are born of the Washington race:
> And this land is the Free America—
> And this mark on my wrist, (I prove what I say)
> Ropes tied me up here to the flogging-place.
>
> (Barrett Browning 1995: 373)

Ina Beth Sessions's pioneering classification of the dramatic monologue identifies seven main characteristics: 'speaker, audience, occasion, revelation of character, interplay between speaker and audience, dramatic action, and action which takes place in the present' (Sessions 1947: 508). This clearly emphasises that the speaker is completely separate from the poet. Langbaum argues that Victorian poets write a lyric of experience in the voice of a character; the reader may identify with the speaker's feelings, but that voice is heard at one remove (Langbaum 1957: 12). Poems such as Tennyson's 'Tithonus', 'Tiresias' and 'Ulysses', Robert Browning's 'Fra Lippo Lippi' or 'The Bishop Orders His Tomb at Saint Praxed's Church' present figures from history and myth. This establishes a distance between the poet and the text, and would appear to replicate the gap between the remote creatures, nature-spirits and abstractions invoked by the Romantic apostrophe, and the 'I' who vainly seeks intimacy with them. Yet the speaker of the Victorian dramatic monologue addresses human auditors, and to some extent 'domesticates' the relationship between speaker and addressee. As W. David Shaw comments, the vocative is the 'defining trope' of Victorian dramatic monologue, which revolves around 'a speaker's seduction of a silent listener' (Shaw 1997: 308).

While the dramatic monologue is associated primarily with the Victorian period, the term was coined only in the later nineteenth century. Many poets instead used phrases such as 'psychological monologues'. Browning preferred the term 'dramatic lyric'. His first collection of monologues was titled *Dramatic Lyrics* (1842), and in the advertisement to the first edition he defined the poems as 'though for the most part Lyric in expression, always Dramatic in principle, and so many utterances of so many imaginary persons, not mine' (Browning 1988: 178). As we saw in Chapter 2, the New Critics argued that all poems contain dramatic features, with the poet adopting an assumed character and position. Ralph Rader, however, has distinguished between dramatic monologues and dramatic lyrics: '[in dramatic monologues] the reader must imagine the speaker as an outward presence, as we in our bodies register others in their bodies, from the outside in, whereas in the dramatic lyric we are imaginatively conflated with the speaker, understanding him from the inside out, seeing with his eyes and speaking with his voice as if on our behalf'. In dramatic lyric, rather than seeing the speaker, we see 'an outward scene that he is understood as seeing, with the camera implicitly taken as our eyes' (Rader 1984: 104). This constructed familiarity, which persuades the reader to identify or sympathise with the speaker, is counterpointed by the unsettled nature of the 'I' in Browning's monologues. As Glennis Byron observes: 'While the lyric "I" is supposed to inspire the reader's confidence in the voice that speaks, in all these poems the authority, integrity and autonomy of that isolated lyric voice are put into question' (Byron 2003: 38).

Browning's 'My Last Duchess' (Browning 1988: 186–88) is regarded as the epitome of the dramatic monologue, and it places the lyric voice under severe interrogation. Indeed, the self-absorption of the speakers in many of Browning's monologues might be regarded as a criticism of the 'wordsworthian or egotistical sublime' anatomised by Keats earlier in the century. In 'My Last Duchess', the Duke of Ferrara is presented as an egomaniac and, implicitly, a murderer. These revelations emerge, however, in a meeting with an agent of the Count of Tyrol, whose daughter the

Duke is seeking to marry. The ostensible business is to fix the financial arrangements – which are dealt with in a few lines towards the end of the poem – but the main drama of the poem lies in the Duke's account of his 'last' Duchess. The portrait that he uncovers shows his former wife as if still alive, but the Duke ruthlessly controls access to her image in the present, just as, the poem implies, he tried to do when she lived. There are strong hints about their relationship, and his jealousy and paranoia: 'her looks went everywhere', 'She thanked men – good!' His aristocratic hauteur would persuade the agent that he is the wounded party, and thus a perfectly good match for the Count's daughter, but there is plenty in the poem to suggest he is far from an ideal husband. There is a particularly sinister implication in the way that the Duchess's 'smiles stopped together' after the Duke 'gave commands', although he has previously claimed that he would never 'stoop' to alter her behaviour. Thus we have a central contradiction in the poem: the Duke uses his rhetorical powers to convince the agent of his suitability – he speaks as one man to another, and despite his pride he is punctiliously polite and solicitous – but the barely concealed anger in his account of his former marriage subverts. This is far from a gentle 'seduction': the Duke's overbearing personality is revealed in his urgent appeal to his silent listener. A variety of devices – mimicry of others' speech, run-on lines, dramatic emphases, rhetorical questions – imitate the patterns of conversational speech, but any notions of sincerity and authenticity are subverted by the power of language to speak over 'against the speaker' (Bristow 1987: 5). There is what we might call a double invitation in this poem: to sympathise with the Duke, and to pass negative judgement. As such, the dramatic monologue asks us to do something, to participate, to evaluate the words we hear, just as we might respond to a speech by a character in a play. So, even if we accept the 'fiction' of the speaking voice, as Paul de Man suggests, this is where the difficulties of interpretation begin. 'My Last Duchess' is a poem about interpretation; the Duke asks the agent to 'read' the Duchess's portrait, to try and understand his feelings. But to understand the Duke's feelings, we have to accept his version of the Duchess, and he admits that he could not comprehend her when she was alive. But is this what the Duke wants the agent, and in turn, the reader, to think? Is he being open, honest, or putting on a public display? We need therefore to think about the dramatic monologue as a rhetorical performance, rather than as a revelation of character.

'My Last Duchess' constructs a character that seems entirely separable from the Romantic lyric 'I', who is typically identified with the empirical writer 'behind' the poem. The dramatic quality of Browning's poem, and its presentation of a speaker who is at one remove from the poet, is made explicit. Yet this is not common to all dramatic monologues or dramatic lyrics in the period. Many of these present less clearly defined characters that shift uncertainly between first and third person perspectives. Alan Sinfield describes this uncertainty within the dramatic monologue as a 'feint'. He argues that dramatic monologue 'lurks provocatively' between the first-person lyric, which gives 'the illusion at least of direct access to the experiencing poet', and the third-person narrative, which posits both a figure describing and a figure being described (Sinfield 1977: 24). In 'My Last Duchess', the feint approximates to fiction, since no reader would mistake the Duke for the 'personal' lyric voice, whereas the feint moves towards the poetic 'I' in Matthew Arnold's 'Dover Beach' (Arnold 1979: 254–56), where there are few signals that the poet is not the speaker. Rader argues that a dramatic lyric such as 'Dover Beach' can be related imaginatively to the reader's experience because it uses 'cinematic' identification, and the speaker becomes 'an ideal extension of the reader's own voice' (Rader 1976: 134). We see directly through the speaker's eyes, rather than observing a character in a dramatic monologue that is separate from our point of view. In the dramatic lyric 'the figure in the poem is imagined by the poet from within, so that we participate in his mental activity as if his eyes and experience had become the poet's and our own' (*ibid.*: 142). In effect, the speaker seems to experience the world in the same way as the reader.

'Dover Beach' works hard to encourage the reader to share its assumptions: it seems more like a private meditation than a conversation, but relies on rhetorical address and persuasion. The poem exhibits the main features of the greater lyric, blending topographical description and philosophical contemplation. It begins in the manner of the place poem:

> The sea is calm tonight.
> The tide is full, the moon lies fair
> Upon the straits – on the French coast the light
> Gleams and is gone; the cliffs of England stand
> Glimmering and vast, out in the tranquil bay.

The text then switches to the vocative, addressing its silent auditor in dramatic terms: 'Listen! you hear the grating roar'. The 'I' next announces itself by adopting the elevated register of the ode to reflect on the 'melancholy, long, withdrawing roar' of the 'Sea of Faith', as the landscape takes on symbolic significance. The silent listener – a spouse or lover – implies a sense of connection and intimacy amidst the 'sadness' and isolation felt by the speaker, but this comfort is rather ambiguous:

> Ah, love, let us be true
> To one another! for the world, which seems
> To lie before us like a land of dreams,
> So various, so beautiful, so new,
> Hath really neither joy, nor love, nor light,
> Nor certitude, nor peace, nor help for pain.

The lover is invoked as a counterpoint to the darkness and isolation of 'ignorant armies' who clash beyond the English channel, but this addressee resembles a forlorn afterthought or rhetorical gambit, rather than a consoling presence. The uncertainty of private love appears merely to confirm the speaker's perception of cultural and political crisis.

It can be argued, then, that the Romantic lyric 'I' was modified rather than erased in Victorian poetic practice. A number of poets produced autobiographical lyric sequences, including George Meredith's *Modern Love* (1862) and Dante Gabriel Rossetti's *The House of Life* (1870/1881). Both Barrett Browning's *Aurora Leigh* and Tennyson's *In Memoriam* are long poems that contain lyric 'interludes'. Tennyson's *In Memoriam* is a lyric sequence rather than a sustained narrative, and the poem is constructed by 'an accretion of moments' (Sacks 1985: 168). The formal features of the poem, such as the slow accumulation of details, disjointed, self-enclosed fragments and resistance to narrative progression, are reflective of melancholia, as Sacks has argued (*ibid.*: 169), and are also indicative of lyric itself. Yet the poem's intense interludes, the suspension of time that fights mortality and transience, are framed by the duration of Hallam's life. In Section 7, this lyric suspension is broken by the passage of time and the intrusion of the outside world, but also by the reluctantly acknowledged absence of the beloved other:

> Dark house, by which once more I stand
> Here in the long unlovely street,
> Doors, where my heart was used to beat
> So quickly, waiting for a hand,
> A hand that can be clasped no more –
> Behold me, for I cannot sleep,
> And like a guilty thing I creep
> At earliest morning to the door.
> He is not here; but far away
> The noise of life begins again,
> And ghastly through the drizzling rain
> On the bald street breaks the blank day.
>
> (Tennyson 1989: 351–52)

Unlike 'I Wandered Lonely' or 'Tintern Abbey', the past is no refuge from the 'unlovely street', and the offered hand that abolishes death in Keats's 'This Living Hand' cannot be clasped.

This inability to vocalise the other is echoed at the end of the century by Thomas Hardy's 'The Darkling Thrush' (Hardy 1923: 137). Like many Romantic place-poems, 'The Darkling Thrush' is precisely dated as being written in December 1900. This act of dating, however, emphasises that the poem marks the 'death' of the nineteenth century, a sense of ending manifest in the spectral midwinter scene. The ghostly lyric 'I' surveys a landscape that no longer provides inspiration, solace or instruction. Nature refutes the poetic impulse – 'tangled bine-stems scored the sky/ Like strings of broken lyres' – and every 'spirit' in this wintry scene is as 'fervourless' as the speaker. The 'overheard' lyric voice of the 'aged' thrush bespeaks 'joy illimited', but the speaker remains unaware of any 'blessed Hope' this voice transmits. Like Wordsworth's Solitary Reaper, Shelley's Skylark or Keats's Nightingale, the thrush's song remains remote and unfathomable, but on this occasion it does not elevate the listener. The failure to participate in or emulate that song is foregrounded rather than denied by Hardy's poem, and the loss and distance that haunts the vocative Romantic lyric becomes acute. The 'I' appeals to a natural world that may not return its call, speaks without passionate immediacy, and recollects emotion as if posthumously.

MODERNISM: THE POETRY OF THINGS

The previous section explored the poetic complex relation between the self and textual personae in Victorian dramatic monologue and dramatic lyric, and modernist poetry further complicates the process of 'speaking through' another, whether it be through a persona, mask, symbol or object. In a modernist dramatic lyric such as T. S. Eliot's 'The Love Song of J. Alfred Prufrock' (Eliot 1985: 13–17), the speaker is both the point of identification and a separate character (or range of personae). Rader terms this elusive figure 'an artificial person projected from the poet, a mask through which he speaks' (Rader 1976: 140). In mask lyrics, 'the mask figure mediates between the poet's private feeling and the reader', and speaker is displayed 'against a manifestly factitious backdrop, a montage of indistinct and fluidly shifting scenes whose very lack of concreteness would be taken as a sign of their expressive artificiality; the scene would be not so much real as surreal' (*ibid*.: 141). 'Prufrock' opens with a seductive, but disconcerting, invitation to the reader: the suggested intimacy between the 'you' and 'I', and the amatory implications of the love song, are undercut by a startling image of dissection. The 'half-deserted' streets are recognisable but they also frustrate attempts to make sense of the sensual and erotic spaces of the city. Its alleyways and retreats become a maze or labyrinth of erotic possibility and sinister threat. The urban space that the protagonist inhabits is not sharply delineated and, like the Romantic place-poem, 'Prufrock' surveys an interior landscape. The poem moves cinematically, voyeuristically through the streets, but this mobility does not comfortably situate the reader. Any progress is thwarted by repetition and hesitation, and the reader becomes enmeshed in the speaker's alienation.

Rader also argues that in the dramatic lyric and the dramatic monologue, the reader participates in the dramatic actor's performance; in the mask lyric, the poet speaks through an actor 'who is registered almost overtly as an artificial self' (*ibid.*: 150). Prufrock — if it is he who speaks throughout the poem — draws attention to his fastidious appearance, and alludes fitfully to an 'external' world, but his reflections are saturated with quotations and allusions and he is constantly assuming disguise after disguise: Lazarus, John the Baptist, figures from literature and myth (Hamlet, Polonius), an insect wriggling on a pin, or a crab on the bottom of the ocean. Eliot's lyric 'I' is characterised by anonymity and disguise, and the mode of address resembles ventriloquism, rather than spontaneous self-expression. Langbaum comments that if we remove or ignore the speaker's immediate situation, 'Prufrock' must be regarded as a traditional lyric that involves retrospection and meditation rather than the 'dramatic presentation' of the speaker's self-realisation (*ibid.*: 157). Yet the 'immediate situation' is crucial for poems such as 'Prufrock', 'Rhapsody on a Windy Night' or 'Preludes'. As their speakers await the 'last twist of the knife' (Eliot 1985: 28), or 'prepare a face' (*ibid.*: 14) to meet the faces in the street, the poems draw attention to social life as a self-conscious performance or masquerade. Given Prufrock's adoption of masks, the text stages his self-concealment rather than his self-realisation. There is another world, the chaotic stimuli of the metropolis, to which the lyric 'I' seems opposed, but to which it is perfectly fitted in its modern form. It is able to compress time and space, and to accommodate the discontinuity and fragmentation of advanced modernity, by arresting the moment and isolating it in startling detail.

In 'The End of the Line' (1942) Randall Jarrell notes this ability as a major characteristic of modernist poetry: 'A great emphasis on details – on parts, not wholes. Poetry is essentially lyric: the rare narrative or expository poem is a half-fortuitous collocation of lyric details' (cited by Cook 2000: 272). Any textual unity achieved is only provisional: this is evident in the shifting locations and voices in the mask lyric, and in the fleeting snapshots provided by Imagism. F. S. Flint's foundational rules for Imagist poetry, published in *Poetry* magazine in March 1913, stress '[d]irect treatment of the "thing", whether subjective or objective', and the avoidance of any word 'that did not contribute to the presentation' (cited by Jones 1972: 129). In the same issue, Ezra Pound's 'A Few Don'ts By An Imagiste' defines the image as 'that which presents an intellectual and emotional complex in an instant of time' (*ibid.*: 130). Pound enjoins the aspiring poet to '[u]se no superfluous word, no adjective which does not reveal something ... Go in fear of abstractions ... Use either no ornament or good ornament' (*ibid.*: 131). The emphasis is on rigour, economy and precision: Imagism is a lyric poetry of hard, clear definition that presents an effulgent snapshot or epiphany captured from the flux, rapidity and shock of the modern. For all its stress on novelty and iconoclasm, however, Imagism reiterates the traditional view that in lyric poetry 'only the great moment exists' (Lukács 1978: 63), and Pound's complex 'strives towards an ideal simultaneity of meaning' (Brooks 1984: 20). H. D.'s extraordinary 'Oread', a whirl of turbulent movement that displaces the boundaries between subject and object, is a startling example of the Imagist aspiration to this simultaneity. May Sinclair declared in 1915 that 'in no case is the Image a symbol of reality (the object); it is reality (the object) itself' (Sinclair 1915: 88). The image thus seeks to collapse the distinction between the world and the word, signifier and signified, in the same manner as the high-flown Romantic ode.

Pound's 'In a Station of the Metro' (Jones 1972: 95) is the paradigmatic Imagist poem. Like the traditional modern lyric, it relates a single image, impression or feeling with directness and brevity. The compression of the scene mirrors the compression of detail in the poem: in two lines the text arrests the speed and accumulation of people in the Paris Underground. The singular faces observed by the speaker resemble 'petals', but it is technological innovation and urban development, rather than natural beauty, that provokes this visual image. The Imagist vision is striking and sudden, but it is also characterised by stillness. Pound's account of the poem's genesis prioritises aesthetic composition: 'Three years ago in Paris I got out of a "metro" train at La Concorde, and saw suddenly a beautiful face, and then another and another, and then a beautiful child's face, and then another beautiful woman' (cited by Thacker 1993: 236). Several features link the poem and Pound's account: the voyeuristic gaze, detachment from the anonymous mass, and the relationship between mobility and stability. Yet 'In a Station of the Metro' leaves the speaker's relationship and attitude to the crowd unstated. Instead of capturing the beauty of the faces, the poem presents them as an 'apparition', suggesting a supernatural encounter. The aestheticisation of the scene thus represents an escape, rather than a direct treatment, of the modern world. Its lyric 'time' is 'outside ordinary duration' and manifests an inner self that can transcend the material world (Middleton and Woods 2000: 73).

Many of the Imagist anthologies were published during the First World War, a period that prompted a massive rise in the production of public, lyric, poetry. The Great War became a test case for how lyric poetry might 'negotiate historical crisis' (Longley 2005: 57). The success of Rupert Brooke's sonnet 'The Soldier' demonstrated how a lyric poem could be exploited for propaganda purposes. It was given poignancy and potency by Brooke's death on a troopship bound for Gallipoli, turning him into the Romantic hero–artist. Yet the modern lyric has been viewed as an inadequate medium to deal with warfare. John H. Johnston argues that in the Victorian period, the lyric surrendered its 'comprehensive vision' to the novel and had become exclusively concerned with 'the expression of personal attitudes' (Johnston 1964: 78). The 'lyric impulse', grounded in 'limited emotional reactions' (*ibid.*: 337), lacked the sense of 'epic' proportion to tackle the realities of a modern conflict. A prominent pre-war model of lyric, Georgian poetry, offered an idyllic view of a pre-industrial, pastoral England that was shattered by the carnage of the trenches. The Prefatory note to the first Georgian anthology, edited by Edward Marsh in 1912, claimed that it showed English poetry 'once again putting on new strength and beauty' (Reeves

1981: xii). Yet Georgian poetry has been somewhat unfairly identified with sentimental escapism: the five Georgian anthologies featured writers such as Siegfried Sassoon and Isaac Rosenberg, whose war poems demythologise notions of noble, patriotic sacrifice. Rosenberg's 'Dead Man's Dump' (Rosenberg 1979: 109–11) uses many features of the modern lyric to convey in graphic detail the experience of frontline troops. It opens as a place-poem: 'The plunging limbers over the shattered track/ Racketed with their rusty freight.' Strikingly, however, the nightmarish situation is articulated through a collective voice rather than a particularised speaker. The poem's rhetorical style and heightened language recall the ode, but the insistent questioning is directed to an uncertain addressee: 'What fierce imaginings their dark souls lit?/ Earth! have they gone into you?' At times the detail is precise and graphic – 'Burnt black by strange decay/ Their sinister faces lie;/ The lid over each eye' – but at other moments the meditative register and inversions counter this immediacy. These modifications show the traditional lyric adjusting to unprecedented subject matter. As Edna Longley suggests, it might be more useful to view First World War lyrics in terms of their ability to 'internalize' history as new formal 'complications' (Longley 2005: 77).

It can be argued that the clinical precision and emotional coolness demanded by the Imagist movement was, in part, a poetic reaction to the clamour and chaos of mechanised slaughter. In Richard Aldington's 'Sunsets' (1916), the evening's 'white body' is 'torn into scarlet,/ Slashed and gouged and seared/ Into crimson', and wind that blows from Flanders to London carries a 'bitter taste' (Jones 1972: 55–56). Aldington, one of the founders of Imagism, served at the front, and his poem 'Living Sepulchres' (57–58) tests Imagist doctrine against the 'thing' it depicts. The poet composes '*hokku*/ Of the moon and flowers and of the snow' when the guns fall silent, but this lyric beauty must compete with the vision of huge rats swollen with men's flesh. H. D. harnesses the power of the image to condemn by implication the masculinism that is intimately linked with militarism and destructive ambitions. In her translation of Euripides's *Iphegeneia in Aulis*, she has the Chorus of the Women of Chalkis view with ambivalence the 50 'quivering' ships of Achilles that are bound for the siege of Troy: 'This beauty is too much/ For any woman./ It is burnt across my eyes' (Jones 1972: 69). Here Greek myth is used 'to confront feminine experience, and to express it in direct opposition to the predominant masculine ideology – an ideology that oppressed women and promoted war' (Collecott 1985: 8–9).

The concentration, restraint and stillness that Imagism espouses is also evident in much of the best known lyric poetry of the Great War, even in the work of writers who were not involved in the movement. Edward Thomas's lyric understatement in a poem such as 'The Cherry Trees' magnifies the noises-off of devastating conflict: the focus remains on the trees' petals, which cover the grass 'as for a wedding/ This early May morn when there is none to wed' (Thomas 1985: 49). 'The Owl' recounts a night journey through a cold landscape, with the voice of the owl 'Speaking for all those who lay under the stars,/ Soldiers and poor, unable to rejoice' (*ibid.*: 26). The impact of the war is measured by changes to rural life: in 'As the Team's Head Brass', a ploughman speculates on the work he would have done had his friend not been killed on his second day in France. Ivor Gurney's 'To His Love' also laments the dead through a retreat to pastoral:

> Cover him, cover him soon!
> And with thick-set
> Masses of memoried flowers–
> Hide that red wet
> Thing I must somehow forget.
>> (Gurney 2004: 21)

In contrast, Wilfred Owen's poems are often rhetorical or dramatic, as in 'Dulce et Decorum Est' or 'Strange Meeting', while others such as 'Anthem for Doomed Youth' are elegiac poems of occasion.

'Prufrock' brings together different strands of the modernist lyric: the mask lyric, Imagism and the meditative sequence. Eliot's 'The Three Voices of Poetry' replaces the term lyric with 'meditative verse', as the OED's definition of lyric is deemed to be inadequate (Eliot 1990: 96–97). The meditative lyric, in which the self becomes the centre of the text (Johnson 1982: 7), can be seen as the successor of the greater Romantic lyric. Yet this self is often marginal or concealed: the 'I' in H. D.'s long poems is installed within an elaborate mythical framework, and Pound's 'E. P. Ode Pour L'Election de son Sepulchre', from *Hugh Selwyn Mauberley* (1920), plays with the authorial name only to mockingly celebrate the inauthenticity of the modern age. In *The Waste Land* (Eliot 1985: 63–86), there is a pervasive narrative I/ eye, akin to the voyeuristic observer of 'Prufrock'. The first person singular is used over 30 times, and each character's dialogue is rendered grammatically distinct by the use of inverted commas, but the 'I' sits indistinctly between a localised and unifying centre of consciousness. Eliot's own notes hint that Tiresias is the 'most important personage in the poem, uniting all the rest' (*ibid.*: 82), but critics have dismissed this persona as 'a mythological catch-all, and as a unifying factor of no effect whatever' (Hough 1960: 25). Tiresias – bisexual, blind, omniscient and immortal – supposedly offers a transhistorical, authoritative perspective, but this androgynous figure drifts in and out of the text. Crucially, s/he embodies the poem's failure of vision: in 'The Fire Sermon', Tiresias has 'foresuffered all', but the nature of that 'all' remains oblique. *The Waste Land* not only challenges the reader to make sense of its anxious meditations; the text itself seems preoccupied with the very possibilities of comprehending a world that appears in apparently disconnected snapshots. The poem's speakers are unable to connect with the modern world, or to assemble its fragments. The citations from classical and modern literature, and the prophetic voice of the closing lines, are yet more disguises and evasions.

The anonymous, detached, elusive speaker who hides behind myths, masks and personae is indicative of the modernist poetics of impersonality. Jon Cook has characterised the twentieth-century lyric as a battleground between personality and impersonality (Cook 2004: 4). In 1950, Charles Olson urged poets to rid poetry of the 'lyrical interference of the individual as ego, of the "subject" and his soul' (cited by *ibid.*: 9), a rejection of the Romantic overheard lyric. Roland Barthes later argues that modern poetry has 'destroyed relationships in language and reduced discourse to words as static things ... modern poetry is a poetry of the object'

(Barthes 1993: 59). This poetry of the object recalls the Anglo-Saxon riddle, but the modern lyric is not the indirect voice of an enigmatic object, as in Craig Raine's Martian poems later in the century: it is the voice of something (language, modernity) rather than someone. The depersonalisation of lyric was taken up as an aesthetic strategy in the Modernist period. Guillaume Apollinaire's 'The New Spirit and the Poets' (1917) announces a 'new spirit [that] admits even hazardous literary experience, and those experiences are at times anything but lyric'. This new lyricism can extend to 'mechanized' art epitomised by the cinema and the 'phonograph', and constitutes a move away from the sincerity, purity and high seriousness associated with the traditional lyric (cited by Cook 2004: 78). Filippo Marinetti's 'Technical Manifesto of Futurist Literature' (1912) espouses a poetry of the machine, 'the dance of an object that divides and recomposes without human intervention' (*ibid.*: 59). Marinetti seeks to 'substitute for human psychology, now exhausted, the lyric obsession with matter' (Marinetti 1972: 87). William Carlos Williams declared that there was 'no poetry but in things' (Williams 1967: 390), an aesthetic epitomised by a poem such as 'The Red Wheelbarrow', an object of simplicity and utility on which 'so much depends' (Moore 1983: 264).

In his 1914 essay 'Vorticism', Pound reflects on the escape from personality in his poetry:

> In the 'search for oneself', in the search for 'sincere self-expression', one gropes, one finds some seeming verity. One says 'I am' this, that, or the other, and with the words scarcely uttered one ceases to be that thing. I began this search for the real in a book called *Personae*, casting off, as it were, complete masks of the self in each poem. I continued in a long series of translations, which were but more elaborate masks.
>
> (Pound 1970: 85).

This 'I' is a provisional, textual construction, not the presiding genius of the Romantic lyric. In 'Tradition and the Individual Talent' (1919), Eliot dismisses Wordsworth's formulation that poetry originates from 'emotion recollected in tranquillity'. The artistic process 'is a continual extinction of personality', and poetry is an 'escape' from, rather than a release of, emotion (Kolocotroni *et al.*, 1998: 369, 370). This depersonalisation is described through a scientific analogy: the poet's mind is likened to 'a shred of platinum' in a catalyst, remaining 'inert, neutral and unchanged' while it transmutes personal thoughts and passions into impersonal art (*ibid.*: 369). Eliot's concept of impersonality nonetheless puts personality centre stage in modernist lyric. As Maud Ellmann comments, Eliot's and Pound's poetry 'should be regarded neither as their mirror nor their hiding-place, but as the laboratory for their fabrication of themselves' (Ellmann 1987: 198).

The depersonalisation of modern lyric, according to Paul de Man, begins with Baudelaire (de Man 1983: 172). In Baudelaire's poetry, the Parisian *flâneur*, the dandified stroller of the city streets, becomes a self-conscious outsider. As Walter Benjamin observes in his influential analysis of the *flâneur*, '[i]nterpersonal relationships in big cities are distinguished by a marked preponderance of the activity of the eye over the ear' (Benjamin 1983: 38). The lyric gaze glimpses isolated fragments, in keeping with the episodic rhythms of the street. The poet is a 'ragpicker' (*ibid.*: 80), a sifter of the city's debris: the movement of the boulevard, its transient novelty and fleeting sensory stimuli, becomes a new subject in lyric poetry. In contrast to the static, contemplative look in the Romantic ode or greater lyric, the modernist gaze is fleeting and furtive, mimicking the restless mobility of urban modernity. The lyric moment is now characterised by collisions and chance encounters that allow the 'I' only a temporary vantage point. The detachment of the lyric 'I' is exacerbated by the sense of poetry's marginalisation in the modern world. While this marginalisation seems to confirm Baudelaire's view that the modern is 'antilyrical' (Adorno 1974: 44), the provocative challenge to the staleness of everyday language, to mass culture and to bourgeois attitudes in the modernist lyric suggests confrontation with, rather than evasion of, this inhospitable climate. For Theodor Adorno, the very possibility of a modern lyric voice 'implies a protest against a social situation that every individual experiences as hostile, alien, cold, oppressive' (*ibid.*: 39).

In the 1930s, the engaged modernism of Pound and Auden – at different ends of the ideological spectrum – returned to 'the historically responsive and dialogical mode' (Tucker 1985: 239): Auden's 'Spain 1937', for example, adopts the 'Horatian' model to present a poem of occasion. Yet modernist poetry engages with the historical moment predominantly through the individual perspective, and modernist lyrics might be approached in terms of the dual poles of modern poetic theory represented by the French poets Arthur Rimbaud and Stéphane Mallarmé. Rimbaud proposes lyric as a realm decisively 'other' than, and actively opposed to, banal bourgeois life, whereas Mallarmé sees lyric as an eternal moment, 'always other and always beyond' the everyday (Grady 1981: 553). These tendencies are not mutually exclusive, however: neither aspires to reflect the world faithfully, and both aim to resist, defamiliarise and transform it. We might cite the example of the Russian poet Marina Tsvetaeva. Her contention that '[p]ure lyric poetry has no project ... [it] is solely the record of our dreams and feelings' (cited by Cook 2004: 217), appears to endorse the Mallarmé version of lyric that lies eternally beyond the world. Yet Tsvetaeva is writing in 1935 during Stalin's reign of terror, when 'dreams and feelings' had to remain utterly hidden from public scrutiny. In this context, the private, disengaged lyric can be seen not just as a refuge, but as a form of defiance to an oppressive social and political situation.

AFTER MODERNISM: PERFORMING THE SELF

To focus the discussion of poetry in the past 50 years, this section concentrates on four main trends within lyric practice: the 'well made' poem; confessional poetry; the dramatic lyric; and innovative poetics. The well made lyric is primarily a poem of experience that maintains a unity of tone and feeling to express a coherent poetic voice. Robert Sheppard terms this forging of poetic identity 'Empirical Lyricism': 'the solitary figure approaches an object or person with awe, only to be deflected or disappointed, before strategic withdrawal and some minute change in the narrator's belief systems. It is the blueprint for thousands of post-war poems' (cited by Brown 2006: 11). Two examples to illustrate this version of lyric will suffice. In Wordsworthian vein, Seamus Heaney's 'Personal Helicon' imaginatively relives a child's experience of gazing at his reflection in wells. This narcissism anticipates the adult practice of poetry, in which the speaker rhymes to 'see myself, to set the darkness echoing' (Heaney 1966: 44). The pleasure and unpredictability of lyric compensates for the loss of innocence and youthful wonder. In Philip Larkin's 'Church Going' (Larkin 1988: 97–98), the solitary 'I' is apologetic, intruding on the scene only once sure 'nothing' is going on and removing his cycle-clips 'in awkward reverence'. The tone is demotic, the perspective detached, and the sardonic visitor makes no claims to high purpose: this formally conservative poetry of observation and quietude seems far distant from the greater lyric. Yet the speaker off-handedly smuggles in specialist knowledge of 'plate and pyx', and gradually invests the scene with significance. The church's silence is 'unignorable' as it becomes 'a serious house on serious earth', and the casual visit turns into an elegiac meditation on the 'hunger' that remains for spiritual belief in a secular world. As such, 'Church Going' echoes the 'local' poem of the eighteenth century. Equally, it constructs a poetic sensibility elevated beyond the anonymous, secular present. These poems seem to speak for themselves, yet each actively fashions a persona and performs an experience. The lyric 'I' finds itself confirmed through poetry, whether as celebrant in 'Personal Helicon', or as knowing outsider in 'Church Going'.

The self-conscious fashioning and performance of a self is fundamental to confessional poetry. The confessional poem, the main exponents of which were John Berryman, Sylvia Plath, Robert Lowell and Anne Sexton, can be considered a descendant of the mask lyric and its complex interplay of sincerity and irony, authenticity and fabrication. Confessional poetry seems to propose an intimate relation between writing and madness, psychological extremity and self-exposure, and presents a stark contrast to the muted, detached perspective associated with Larkin and others. The confessional poem, like other versions of modern lyric, performs the self, but its construction of subjectivity becomes a poetic process, an act of transformation and disguise, as much as a revelation of the tortured self. Plath, Sexton and Lowell were noted performers of their work, and the elaborate display of feeling in the poetry became interwoven with their public personae. Deryn Rees-Jones argues that we should understand the confessional poem as an act of catharsis. However extreme or transgressive the experience conveyed by the confessional poem, it depends upon a sympathetic union between poet and reader, a kind of understanding and forgiveness: 'More than any other genre, the confessional poem demands a dynamic of belief between reader or listener and poet' (Rees-Jones 2005: 129). The work of exposure and potential healing involves an explicit act of address: there is an exchange between an 'I' and a 'you', rather than an overheard utterance. Yet the calculated nature of this confessional address raises fundamental questions about the authenticity of the textual voice. As Rees-Jones remarks: 'Unlike autobiography, which purports to document factual and emotional truth, and which embeds its "I" within a narrative, confessional poetry hovers in a hinterland between documentary experience and fiction, establishing itself as a mode which draws closer the borders of the relationship between the "I" who speaks and the "I" who is spoken about' (Rees-Jones 2005: 14–15).

The self-conscious interweaving of poetry and mental collapse in Anne Sexton's life and work exemplifies the public construction of confessional poetry. During therapy following her first breakdown, she began to write of her experiences, as if that were part of the treatment. The title of her 1960 collection, *To Bedlam and Part Way Back*, suggests that to confess private difficulties, to show everything, is the legitimate and necessary aesthetic strategy. Jacqueline Rose declares Sexton

> the performance artist of intimacy. Standing before her audience she would, seemingly without inhibition, offer up in her poetry the most private details of her life. It was the great literary roadshow of the unconscious, writing as psychic striptease.
>
> (Rose 2003: 17)

Sexton's macabre version of the fairy tale Sleeping Beauty, 'Briar Rose' (Sexton 1971: 107–12), is a clear illustration of this apparent exhibitionism. The speaker is a 'trance girl' who 'is yours to do with'. Death 'rattles' in her throat but 'You can stick a needle/ through my kneecap and I won't flinch/ I'm all shot up with Novocain'. Yet even in this state of vulnerability and exposure, the 'trance girl' assumes different roles: through a self-consciously theatrical or story-telling element, and the adoption of different voices, the poem makes explicit its concern with the transformation of subjectivity. Sexton, like Plath, uncovers and magnifies post-Second World War myths about domesticity and femininity, producing a nightmarish version of this constrained, sanitised society. The apparent creative 'illness' or vulnerability of these women becomes a critical weapon, rather than a weakness. They are able to play with roles and assume disguises, and to distort and magnify images and perceptions of motherhood and femininity. When Sexton's therapist made transcripts of her sessions publicly available to Sexton's biographer, Diane Middlebrook, nothing seemed to be private or hidden: all was laid bare. Yet in those therapy sessions, Sexton is no more or less revealed than in her poetry, since there are different versions of the confessional self on display. As Sexton remarked, 'I use the personal when I am applying a mask to my face ... I fake it up with the truth'. Her work suggests that 'performed self-exposure may be one of the best ways for poets ... to hide' (Rose 2003: 18).

Similar questions concerning authenticity and revelation are provoked by Plath's notorious 'Daddy' (Plath 1981: 222–24). Her introduction to the poem for a BBC radio broadcast in 1961 suggested its autobiograpical origins: 'Here is a poem spoken by a girl with an Electra complex. Her father died while she thought he was God. Her case is complicated by the fact that her father was also a Nazi and her mother very possibly part-Jewish. In the daughter the two strains marry and paralyse each other – she has to act out the awful little allegory once over before she is free of it' (Plath 1981: 293). Yet to what extent does this account explain or personalise the poem? One cannot readily presume that Plath is actually speaking about herself here, since she places the poem's scenario within the realm of the mythic or fantastic. Neil Roberts remarks that '[r]eading "Daddy" is like observing a psychic drama' (Roberts 1999: 26), but the staging of 'private' distress is highly self-conscious. 'Lady Lazarus', for example, anticipates a readerly response by suggesting that dying is an art and a commodity for the confessional poet, who is less a victim than a performer for an audience.

'Daddy' is a dramatic monologue, or series of monologues, where the speaker inhabits a range of roles and voices that both identify with and attack the father figure. (We briefly return to 'Daddy' as a strange amalgam of elegy and the conventional love poem in Chapter 5.) A poem of personal revelation or testimony depends on the reader's estimation of its sincerity, and since Wimsatt's and Beardsley's attack on the intentional fallacy, we approach the text's claims with scepticism. Jonathan Holden reminds us, however, that it remains difficult to avoid making assumptions about 'about the human voice behind the printed page' (Holden 1981: xv). In a poem such as 'Daddy', where the simulation of psychic extremity makes reading an uncomfortable process, the persona might be regarded as a necessary fiction. It does not provide an unexpurgated account of Sylvia Plath's mental distress, but it does negotiate ideological contradictions through fantasy scenarios and the adoption of masks.

Marjorie Perloff has questioned the extent to which lyric can still sound 'natural' or authentic in a world of VCRs, iPods, computer games, web-based media and other forms of digital technology (Cook 2004: 547). In this context, terms such as immediacy and sincerity become problematic. Yet the element of performance remains strong in contemporary poetry, whether in the form of performance poetry, or in its use of dramatised speakers. Tony Harrison's poetry deploys both the dramatic monologue and mask lyrics in which several different versions of the self are presented. 'Them and [uz] I & II' (Harrison 1987: 122–23), which stages a debate about the proper voice of (lyric) poetry and its 'high' and 'low' purposes, presents two selves that are continually in conflict. In the first of the two Meridithian sonnets that make up the poem, the Leeds dialect of a schoolboy who recites Keats's 'Ode to a Nightingale' ('mi 'art aches') is juxtaposed with a voice of cultural authority, his teacher, who pronounces that poetry is 'the speech of kings'. In the latter sonnet, however, the humiliated schoolboy has become a double-voiced speaker who commands both elevated poetic language and an irreverent vernacular tongue that challenges the hierarchical assumptions articulated in the classroom. The speaker cites two examples of canonical poets, Wordsworth and Keats, whose work serves to question the 'natural' dominance of received pronunciation and standard English in the study and reception of English literature. 'Cockney' Keats was attacked by Byron and others for his class background, while Wordsworth's poetic voice was shaped by Cumbrian dialect: his 'water' rhymed with 'matter'. The poem is partly dedicated to the comedian Leon Cortez, who was famous for linguistically mangling literary classics, deliberately misappropriating 'high' culture, not through ignorance but through self-conscious irony.

This dialogical strategy is sharply illustrated in the long poem *V* (235–49), which was given an added performance dimension when filmed by Channel 4. The speaker's elegiac meditation on his parents' vandalised gravestones in Leeds is interrupted by a skinhead who is presented as the poet's *alter ego*. These poetic dialogues possess the politicised dimension noted earlier in the discussion of Victorian dramatic monologue, yet it is all-too inviting to align the real, empirical Tony Harrison with the poetic persona his work constructs. In *V*, the poet deploys Rimbaud's statement *'Je est un autre'* ('I is an other') to tackle his internal 'skinhead' voice: 'the skin and poet united fucking Rimbaud/ but the *autre* that *je est* is fucking you' (*ibid.*: 242). The unsettling conjunction of a first-person pronoun and a third-person construction suggests a lyric subjectivity that is split rather than unified, a composite of alien and familiar elements. While Harrison's poems appear to convey personal frustration and a sense of social injustice, they chart a generational fracture or tension for children whose educational opportunities moved them beyond a working-class environment but did not remove the guilt and anger this engendered. The divided textual 'I' in Harrison's lyrics embodies this unresolved split, which can be mapped onto a wider social and economic transition within post-war Britain. As such, the highly individualised voice in Harrison's poetry is a representative 'I' whose experience reflects a contested national history.

Carol Ann Duffy is the best known contemporary exponent of the dramatic monologue. Her dramatic monologues are often overtly politicised, and look back to Victorian women poets such as Barrett Browning and Webster. Deryn Rees-Jones comments that 'the dramatic monologue has perhaps appealed to women because of the way it emphasises an artificiality that women already sense in constructions of their own subjectivity' (Rees-Jones 2005: 158). Duffy's monologues feature the socially isolated – immigrants, displaced children – as well as threatening or strange figures, such as the serial killer of 'Psychopath' (Duffy 2006: 43–46), a sinister ventriloquist's dummy and assorted loners. 'Comprehensive' (*ibid.*: 5–7) orchestrates a variety of teenage voices to reflect on cultural differences and racial tensions in modern Britain. Arguably, 'My Last Duchess' is a clear forerunner to Duffy's 'Psychopath', for in Browning's poem, too, we have the words of a misogynistic killer as our point-of-view protagonist. The gender politics of *The World's Wife* (1999) is underscored by humour: the monologues from assertive women hitherto obscured by 'great men', and their attitudes towards their other 'halves', are often parodic and sceptical.

In the past 40 years, a range of poets have exploited the potential of the dramatic lyric to interrogate a history of exclusion and silence on the basis of gender, race or sexuality. The 'I' of Grace Nichols's *Fat Black Women Poems* (1984) is at once a construction of colonial ideology and a subversive challenge to its racist assumptions. This woman speaks, seeks pleasure, rejoices in her physicality and is not reducible to an object of desire or fascinated disgust in the male imagination. In 'Thoughts drifting through the fat black woman's head while having a full bubble bath' (Rees-Jones 2005: 279–80), the racialised term 'steatopygous', which was used to categorise a physical 'deformity' in black women in southern Africa, becomes a celebratory word of imaginative escape: 'Steatopygous sky/ Steatopygous sea/ Steatopygous waves/ Steatopygous me'. History encroaches on this private lyric moment, but it is deliberately engaged rather than evaded. The speaker of John Agard's 'Listen Mr Oxford Don' (Caddel and Quartermain 1999: 4–5) plays with the stereotype of the black street criminal in order to challenge the assumptions of the eponymous academic. The speaker incites 'rhyme to riot', and in a calculated creative assault on poetic tradition makes 'de Queen's English accessory/ to my offence'. The speaker has an intricate appreciation of poetic rhythm and rhyming patterns, and this historical awareness enables a creative break with the inherited conventions of lyric poetry and helps to construct a voice on very different terms.

Such poems expose the textual self as a creature of language and poetic convention, and compose a resistant 'double' voice that is 'other' to the traditional lyric 'I'. This poetics of identity often still depends on the concept of stable selfhood that can speak itself, however. The dominant paradigm for contemporary poetry has become 'the autobiographical poetry of voice, an artifice of expression that depends heavily on its implicit claim to authenticity' (Middleton and Woods 2000: 188). Middleton and Woods stress that autobiographical lyrics draw on 'a cultural pool of identity paradigms', rather than articulating an original, individual voice. They liken personal lyrics of this kind to 'pieces of clothing and jewellery' that 'can be worn by readers who wish to project different identities' (*ibid*.: 201).

Many contemporary poets explore a lyric voice that is fluid and fractured, its subjectivity a product of the slipperiness and duplicity of language. Within a broadly mainstream context, Paul Muldoon's riddling, exorbitant narratives, extravagant verbal play and quirky metamorphic personae dramatize the complex relationship between subjectivity and writing. Jonathan Holden has noted the blurred 'you' deployed in American poetry: this 'you' denotes in turn the reader, a sense of 'one' that links the poet/speaker and the reader, and it also acknowledges that the poet's utterance is being overheard by an audience (Holden 1981: 55). In the field of experimental and linguistically innovative poetry, writers such as J. H. Prynne, John Ashbery, Denise Riley and American-language poets eschew the biographical or psychological depth that typifies the modern lyric 'I'. While there is no independent, pre-given 'self' to present or to overhear in the experimental lyric poem, such poetry does not exclude 'the expressive self', but rather 'gives it full play' (Middleton 1993: 120). This can involve the ironic dramatising of a speaker, the assemblage of heterogeneous fragments of text and image, and the use of unattributable pronouns that deny a single perspective or point of identification for the reader.

Yet the predominance of voiced poems in the contemporary period, and the lingering 'illusion of selfhood' (Mulford 1983: 31), can also be a means of questioning assumptions about the stable lyric 'I'. Linguistically innovative poetry may seek to deconstruct 'the possibility of the formation of a coherent or consistent lyrical voice, a transcendental ego' (Perloff 1990: 12), but for some poets the lyric I remains 'a necessary formulation for asserting a suppressed or erased identity' (Kinnahan 1996: 635). For example, experimental women writers and feminist theorists share a concern with the limitations and possibilities of the lyric 'I' that Helen Kidd articulates:

> If I were to use the subject position 'I' confidently and authoritatively, my words would always begin to sound hollow to me. The implications of fixed authority and all its attendant rhetoric carried by the assertive 'I', leave me feeling that such an attitude begs the presence of the abyss ... underlying the brittle and temporary subject.
>
> (Kidd 1993: 157)

In *The Pink Guitar*, Rachel Blau Du Plessis urges the feminist writer to 'Write several selves to dissolve the bounded idea of the self' (DuPlessis 1990: 149), and the shifting pronouns of Adrienne Rich's 'Diving into the Wreck' (Rees-Jones 2005: 141–43) put in question the concept of a gendered textual 'I': 'We circle silently/ about the wreck/ we dive into the hold./ I am she: I am he' // 'We are, I am, you are'. The pronouns shift between genders, self and other, individuality and commonality; the extract initially seems to affirm shared female experience, but the sudden slippage from 'she' to 'he' suggests that gender is not a matter of rigid designation or exclusion, and that the text constitutes a possible point of identification for female and male readers. The love poem is prime terrain on which to dissolve the 'bounded idea of the self'. If the identity, gender or sexual orientation of the 'I' and the 'you' cannot be taken for granted, the reader is obliged to re-evaluate the traditional power relations that underwrite the love lyric. As Harriet Tarlo argues, the disruption of pronouns, or grammatical 'shifters', forms a 'significant part of the gender and language politics' of feminist theory and experimental poetry (Tarlo 2000: 248).

Denise Riley's poetry brings together these two strands: her philosophical enquiry into the relationship between writing and subjectivity informs her politics. There is a high degree of theoretical self-awareness, particularly in relation to feminist and psychoanalytical thought, in both her poetic and critical practice. In this she follows the example of Veronica Forrest-Thomson, who blended modernist and post-modernist poetic influences with deconstruction and linguistic philosophy in her work. In *The Words of Selves*, Riley rejects the very basis of Romantic lyric in authentic presence: 'What purports to be "I" speaks back to me, and I can't believe what I hear it say ... The strains of describing the self are also acute within those literary genres reliant on a covert self-presentation: hence it is a liar who writes, and a liar who tries lyric' (Riley 2000: 61, 18). Riley seeks to explore the difference between older models of lyric and the 'self-presentation' of the modern period:

> Poetry can be heard to stagger under a weight of self-portrayal, having taken [the self] as its sole and proper object. Today's lyric form, frequently a vehicle for innocuous display and confessionals, is [thus] at odds with its remoter history. What might transpire if this discontinuous legacy in self-telling became the object of a poem itself?
>
> (ibid.: 94)

Riley's 'Lyric' articulates this 'discontinuous legacy'. The 'I', beguiled by the 'music' and 'sweetness' of the lyric, remains centre stage, but it is exposed as a discursive construction: 'Take up a pleat in this awful/ process and then fold me flat/ inside it so that I don't see/ where I was already knotted in' (Riley 1993: 36). The pronoun 'it' refers here to the lyric as a genre, to this specific poem, and to the 'I' it fashions. This can be seen as a more extreme instance of the 'depersonalisation' of lyric discussed earlier in this chapter.

Riley's displacement of the modern lyric 'I' illustrates Andy Brown's contention that '[l]yric poetry has become more than an expression of musical subjectivity hoping to broaden its reference to universal experience'; contemporary lyric has 'come to explore the gaps between *the world as we experience it* and *experience as we describe it*' (Brown 2006: 12). Riley's poetry investigates the 'knotty, endlessly compelling problem' of 'the nature of the self and the speaking "I"' (Broom 2006: 206), and its first person voice never allows the reader to immerse him/ herself in its constructed world. 'Dark Looks' declares that 'Who anyone is or I am is nothing to the work' (Riley 1993: 54) while 'A Misremembered

Lyric' suggests that the lyric self is always outside of 'me', whether this be the writer or the reader: 'Oh and never/ notice yourself ever. As in life you don't' (*ibid.*: 31). Yet the 'experience' to which Brown refers is not to be understood in abstract terms: Carol Watts also notes the 'ventriloquated and dissenting voice' (Watts 2000: 157) that drives Riley's lyric practice. The process of ungrounding or decentring the poetic self actually conveys how ideologically situated, how linguistically constructed, identity is. 'Affections Must Not' (Rees-Jones 2005: 266–67) interrogates the 'old fiction of reliability' that is domesticated femininity: the fiction that stands up in the kitchen may be a 'shelter' from storms, but it can also underpin a master–slave relationship. The text rejects various versions of femininity – wife, mother, lover – and opposes the 'not-me' to the generalisations of 'sociology'. The last line consists of pronoun, verb, definite article and noun, but each word is distinct, left to stand on its own without qualification: 'I. neglect. the. house'. If read as a single sentence, the line is an indictment of domestic failure, or a determined refusal of a woman's typical role. Significantly, the 'I' is separated spatially and grammatically, implying that it is not reducible to a designated social role or subject position.

This discussion has shown that the reflexive, performative modern lyric cannot rely on a stable circuit of communication between speaker and receiver. Our habits of reading persuade us to accept the necessary fiction that a speaker is sharing her/his innermost thoughts and feelings with us. Yet that 'I' who speaks, the 'you' who is addressed, and the relationship between these two figures, are not designated in advance and remain open to question. The lyric should thus be understood as an event of language. The modern lyric is outside of 'me', and however personal it seems, the lyric voice is always heard through another's lips: the text, the persona, the unpredictable movements of language itself.

5

LOVE, LOSS AND THE BEYOND
LYRICS OF DESIRE

As the preceding chapters have shown, lyric has typically taken the form of an expression of love for a corporeal lover or for a transcendent, spiritualised presence. This chapter assesses lyric modes – love poems, elegies and devotional verse – that are animated by yearning or desire in both spiritual and secular guises. The first section traces the development of the love poem from its classical origins through to the modern period. From its earliest moments, the love lyric has tended to 'focus more on the lover than on love itself' (Blevins 2004: 2) and, since the early modern period, it has become acutely self-aware. By exploring the reworking of Petrarchan conventions from the sixteenth and seventeenth centuries through to the contemporary period, the discussion demonstrates that the love lyric has been concerned as much with the poetics of subjectivity as with erotic physicality and emotional attachment. The section also reveals the love poem as an arena in which dominant constructions of gender and sexuality are affirmed and contested. The discussion then examines the affinities between elegy and lyric. These modes share an ancient lineage, in that both involve song and solitary speakers, and their structures of address and expressions of feeling are predicated upon absence or loss. The chapter finally examines the tradition of devotional poetry from the medieval period to the present. It considers how the love poem and religious lyric have often been interwoven and at times mutually reinforcing, whether in the idealising of the lover in the Petrarchan tradition or the eroticisation of spiritual language in devotional verse. The love lyric, the elegy and the religious poem place a textual self in dialogue with the other, whether it be a lover, the dead or the divine, and they often deploy elaborate modes of address in an attempt to bridge the gap between the 'I' and an unattainable presence. From the courtly love sonnet to the hymn and the apostrophe, the lyric mode strives to reach beyond the limits of language, yet it remains anchored in the present moment of its utterance. The enduring power of lyric lies in the way it plays out this tension between the 'here and now' and the timeless.

THE LOVE LYRIC

The love poem is inseparable from the origins of lyric, a connection that can be traced back to the Greek poet Sappho, who wrote on the island of Lesbos in the mid-seventh century BCE. Her poetry now survives only in fragments (in quotations by other ancient writers, and on scraps of papyrus used to wrap dead bodies), but she has become 'the proper name for lyric poetry itself', even though she may have been only a fictional persona (Prins 1999: 8). Sappho establishes the link between lyric and song, and her poetry has provided many of the conventions of the love lyric: praise and idealisation, the power relations that structure sexuality, and the distance between lover and beloved. As Emily Wilson observes: 'The tension between the self who desires and the self who notices ... has been an essential element in the influence of Sappho's poem on later writers of lyric' (Wilson 2004: 31). This tension is a consistent feature of love lyric. Sappho has also been invoked at various times to authorise a female poetic tradition or to affirm lesbian identity, as her love poems are addressed explicitly to women. Indeed, it is partly through Sappho that female homosexuality came to be understood as 'a distinct sexual orientation' (*ibid.*: 31). It has invariably been assumed that the voiceless object or addressee of the love lyric is female, but in Sappho a woman speaks. Her poems, which articulate same-sex desire, also counter the normative assumptions that underpin the love lyric. The fact that some of Shakespeare's sonnets may be addressed to a young man rather than a mistress means that we cannot automatically gender the pronouns 'I' and 'you' in any love poem. Thus the construction of the voice, and the nature of address, in Sappho's poetry are not solely formal concerns: the lyric 'I' cannot be dissociated from questions of gender and sexuality.

This is typified in Sappho's Fragment 16, discovered only in 1906. The poem reflects on the nature of desire, and locates it not in cavalry, infantry or a fleet of ships, but in a vision of the beloved:

> ... [something] now reminds me of Anactoria
> who is not here
> I would rather see her lovely walk
> and the bright lamp of her face
> than Lydian war chariots and full-armed
> footsoldiers
>
> (Prins 1999: 129)

The poem privileges private intimacy over public life. While Anactoria is absent, the memory of her beauty counters the forbidding militaristic spectacle. The poetic moment becomes a means of rethinking the heroic, masculine imperatives of the present. The lyric fragment can therefore be viewed as 'a site of resistance' (Gregory 2003: 24) rather than as escapist or timeless, and recalls H. D.'s ambivalent translation of Greek myth during the early twentieth century. For Eileen Gregory, the heterodox strategies of Sappho and H. D. demonstrate that lyric, far from being divorced from the public sphere, may be 'potentially the most radical and subversive of literary genres' (*ibid.*: 21).

Male poets in the early modern period look back to the classical tradition, but their models are Roman poets such as Ovid and Catullus rather than Sappho. Ben Jonson's 'Song: To Celia' mimics Catullus's 'Lesbia' poems, while Robert Herrick's 'Corinna's Going A-Maying' recalls the mistress of Ovid's love poetry and the *carpe diem* of Horace. Ovid's *Ars Amatoria* underpinned the development of the courtly love lyric, while the *Carmina* of Catullus helped to shape the Petrarchan tradition. The male speakers in Catullus must try to reconcile physical gratification with civic fidelity and duty, just as the subjects in early modern lyrics 'must negotiate their personal needs and desires with neoplatonic and Petrarchan ideals' (Blevins 2004: 4). This is a male classical inheritance: the Lady, the mistress, the Beloved, is generally voiceless and textually absent.

The female voice did speak back, however, in the development of the Petrarchan tradition. Women composed and performed love lyrics in the medieval period, whether in Portugal, France or Al-Andalus. Beatrice, Countess of Die, one of the few women working within the Provençal troubadour tradition, deployed but also challenged the language and generic conventions of the aristocratic, masculine *amour courtois* (Dronke 1968: 105). It is the female lover, or aspirant lover, who speaks in her poems, and it is the male who is objectified. '*Estat ai en gran consirier*/ I have been in great distress' exemplifies the way in which she reverses conventions. The woman is not ethereal, coy or faithless, and she articulates her sexual desire as directly as any male persona:

> I have been in great distress
> for a knight for whom I longed;
> I want all future times to know
> how I loved him to excess.
> Now I see I am betrayed –
> he claims I did not give him love –
> such was the mistake I made,
> naked in bed, and dressed.
> How I'd long to hold him pressed
> naked in my arms one night –
> if I could be his pillow once,
> would he not know the height of bliss?
> Floris was all to Blanchefleur,
> yet no so much as I am his:

> I am giving my heart, my love,
> my mind, my life, my eyes.
> Fair, gentle lover, gracious knight,
> if once I held you as my prize
> and lay with you a single night
> and gave you a love-laden kiss –
> my greatest longing is for you
> to lie there in my husband's place,
> but only if you promise this:
> to do all I'd want to do.
>
> (*ibid.*: 105–06)

Despite the allusion to legendary lovers from medieval romance, directness and reciprocity are the signatures of this poem, which favours physical detail over spiritual abstraction.

This is in marked contrast to the self-conscious display of the courtly love poem as practised by Petrarch and Pierre de Ronsard (1524–85), although it often questions the degree to which perceived reality can match up to the conventions of love. As we saw in Chapter 3, in the Elizabethan Court these conventions were themselves politically charged. The Petrarchan yearning for a remote love object was bound up with worldly concerns relating to patronage and social advancement. In the later medieval period, the idealised female love object of the troubadour and Petrarchan tradition could become the Virgin Mary; in later sixteenth-century England, the unattainable woman whose favour was sought was the Virgin Queen.

The sensuous and erotic origins of Provençal lyric were gradually refined by the codes of feudal service and the idealism of the romance tradition. Earthly, sexual desire was sublimated into spiritual yearning, but in practice the two forms of love were closely linked, with religious concepts lending 'added piquancy' to physical desire (Lever 1956: 2). Wyatt's 'Whoso list to hunt' represents an uneasy mingling of spiritual and physical:

> Whoso list to hunt, I know where is an hind,
> But as for me, alas, I may no more.

The vain travail hath wearied me so sore
I am of them that farthest cometh behind.
Yet may I, by no means, my wearied mind
Draw from the deer, but as she fleeth afore,
Fainting I follow. Leave off therefore,
Since in a net I seek to hold the wind.
Who list to hunt, I put him out of doubt,
As well as I, may spend his time in vain.
And graven with diamonds in letters plain
There is written, her fair neck round about,
'*Noli me tangere*, for Caesar's I am,
And wild for to hold, though I seem tame.'

(Ricks 1999: 28)

The poem is an adaptation of Petrarch's Rime 190, and the Latin
quotation alludes to commentaries of Petrarch, which suggested that
the collars of Caesar's hinds were inscribed with the words '*Noli
me tangere quia Caesaris sum*' ('Do not touch me, for I am Caesar's').
The phrase also has a Biblical register. Its first part recalls Christ's
words to Mary Magdelene in the Garden of Gethsemane, and the
second refers to his remarks about rendering tribute to Caesar.
One allusion gives the woman a high purpose; the other translates
her into material wealth (Heale 1998: 57). The hunted female
figure is taken to refer to Anne Boleyn, second wife of Henry VIII
and mother of Elizabeth I, who was executed for alleged adultery
in 1536, but the deer stands more widely for all women ensnared
in the courtly competition. The hind does not speak the words of
its submission: she is the object of male appetite, and the men's
sexual potency is bound up with the virile activity of the hunt.
The poem excludes the female reader: its implied addressees are
other men who participate in the hunt (*ibid.*: 56). Yet, far from
celebrating the triumph of the male lover/hunter, the poem
records the failure of a chase and the thwarting of desire. Not
only does the speaker fail, it is implied that all hunters will fail.
They are subservient to a greater or transcendent power – the
King, God, the venerated Lady, all objects of desire – and the
hind may never be tamed or possessed. Thus the sonnet conflates
sexual anxieties with frustrations over social hierarchy.

Spenser's *Amoretti* represents the other end of the spectrum. The sequence depicts a courtship in which physical consummation is not a primary goal: the aim is to persuade the lover to marry. Sonnet 75 has none of the immediacy, or unresolved social tensions, of Wyatt's poem, and resembles instead an elegiac apostrophe:

> One day I wrote her name upon the strand,
> But came the waves and washèd it away:
> Again I wrote it with a second hand,
> But came the tide and made my pains his prey.
> 'Vain man', said she, 'that dost in vain essay
> A mortal thing so to immortalize;
> For I myself shall like to this decay,
> And eke my name be wipèd out likewise.'
> 'Not so,' quod I, 'let baser things devise
> To die in dust, but you shall live by fame;
> My verse your virtues rare shall èternize,
> And in the heavens write your glorious name:
> Where, whenas Death shall all the world subdue,
> Our love shall live, and later life renew.'
>
> (Ault 1949: 205)

The pursuit of the idealised other transfigures the poem which, like the immortal love it celebrates, will survive. Through its elevated purpose, the sonnet not only exalts the Beloved but also confirms a poetic identity.

Shakespeare's *Sonnets*, however, return to the bitter disillusionment of Wyatt's poetry. Their subject struggles to define itself 'within an imperfect love' (Blevins 2004: 61), and the mood shifts from idealism to cynicism. In Sonnet 57, the speaker is in thrall to the 'sovereign' Fair Youth: 'Being your slave, what should I do but tend/ Upon the hours and times of your desire?'. The 'I' is aware of the hierarchical and self-deluding nature of the relationship, but is powerless to change the situation: 'So true a fool is love, that in your will,/ Though you do anything, he thinks no ill' (Shakespeare 2006: 55). Sonnet 69, however, acknowledges that the beloved master/mistress is tainted: 'But why thy odour matcheth not thy show,/ This soil is this, that thou dost common grow' (*ibid.*: 61). In Sonnet 137, the Dark Lady's failings are no longer in doubt: 'In things right true my heart and eyes have erred,/ And to this false plague are they now transferred' (*ibid.*: 95). While the voice in Shakespeare's *Sonnets* questions Petrarchan values, its shifting positions and identifications are also a product of those values. As Gary Waller comments, Petrarchism helped 'to articulate a cultural crisis over the nature of the "self" or the "subject" far broader than just the emergence of a "personal" voice in poetry. It also spoke to the emerging consciousness of the "self" as constructed by gender and sexuality' (Waller 1993: 83).

Donne's poetry places this emerging consciousness centre stage. Parfitt suggests that his love lyrics are 'valuable primarily as a sustained explication of male attitudes to women' (Parfitt 1992: 25), but despite the aggressiveness of their erotic vocabulary, the power of the masculine voice is not wholly assured. 'A Valediction Forbidding Mourning' appears to privilege the mobile, assertive male speaker over the silent, passive woman confined to the private realm: the dialogue is one-way, and the suggestion of reciprocity or equality is merely rhetorical. Yet the poem's conceit functions only if there is a mutually dependent relationship between these two figures. Antony Easthope reads 'To his Mistris Going to Bed' (Donne 1985: 183–85) as an instance of male narcissism. The speaker seeks to master the woman with his gaze, desiring 'neither the woman nor sexual satisfaction but rather a transcendent object [that] may return him to an equally perfect reflection of himself' (Easthope 1989: 58). Catherine Belsey argues, however, that nothing sexual happens in the poem: it is 'a text of desire', in which the gaze sees nothing, since desire is 'predicated on absence' (Belsey 1999: 66).

The male voice assumes fluctuating guises in the seventeenth-century love lyric. Donne's directness contrasts starkly with the Cavalier poetry of Lovelace, Suckling and Carew, which transforms the long-suffering or meditative Petrarchan suitor into a witty, courtly lover. Courtship is conducted as a form of gallantry rather than through strenuous philosophical debate or physical aggression. The Caroline lyric, in turn, differs from the sexually graphic and sometimes scatological poetry of the Restoration period. The seduction or *carpe diem* poem replaces the neoplatonic idealism of the courtly lyric, and its elaborate compliments to the ethereal mistress, with a blatant attempt to persuade the actual or potential lover to seize the moment and enjoy physical pleasure. Donne's 'The Relic' and 'The Good Morrow' chart a middle path between a spiritual love that rises above fleshly impulses, and the imperatives of *carpe diem*. 'The Good Morrow' reflects on a higher love, but its reflection is shaped by the aubade, 'a morning serenade of a lover to his mistress' and the aube, 'which presents a conversation between two lovers as they awaken at dawn after a night of love' (Hunt 1954: 54). Marvell's 'To His Coy Mistress' is an exercise in rhetorical display, but the verbal panache of its conceits does not obscure the undercurrent of aggression in the lover's addresses:

> Now let us sport us while we may,
> And now, like amorous birds of prey,
> Rather at once our time devour
> Than languish in his slow-chapped power.
> (Marvell 2003: 50–51)

The enjambment builds the urgency of the appeal, which seeks to 'tear our pleasures with rough strife/ Through the iron gates of life'. Like Browning's 'My Last Duchess', Marvell's dramatic lyric exposes the latent violence of its speaker, and strips away a veneer of gentility and etiquette.

In the later seventeenth century, the poems of female friendship produced by Katherine Philips, Anne Finch, Jane Barker and others adapt courtly love lyrics in a quietly resistant fashion. Their speakers have emotional and intellectual autonomy, and the feelings expressed for other women are both spiritual and erotic. These love poems can be set against the libertine poetry of the Restoration period, in which women are the object of the sexual hunt. Aphra Behn draws on the pastoral mode to question more vigorously 'the unequal play of power in love relations' (Munns 2004: 205) that characterised the amatory lyric. Love of various kinds is celebrated in pastoral lyric: marital or neoplatonic love, friendship between women, homoerotic desire or libertine pleasure. Behn deploys both male and female speakers, and in some cases these voices are not clearly gendered. Her translations of classical poetry rewrite poetic tradition and revise dominant constructions of gender and sexuality. In 'A Voyage to the Isle of Love' (1684), the speaker Lisander recounts his vain pursuit of Aminta to his friend Lycidus. When Aminta finally responds to Lisander's amorous advances, he succumbs to untimely impotence: 'Unable to possess the conquer'd Joys' he sees 'the trembling, dis-appointed Maid,/ With charming angry Eyes my fault up-braid' (Behn 1992: 156). There are multiple humiliations here: Lisander's failure is admitted to an intimate male companion, the traditional direction of gaze is reversed by Aminta's accusing stare, he seems to represent a case of 'all talk, no action' and, shortly after this debacle, Aminta inexplicably dies, putting a stop to any further courtship. Her demise can be read as an indictment of the love lyric, which cannot offer meaningful fulfilment to a woman; equally, however, Behn may be implying that her problems are 'not so much lethal as disappointing' (Munns 2004: 211).

This is made apparent in 'The Disappointment' (1684), a riposte to the libertine Rochester's 'The Imperfect Enjoyment' (1680), where the man reflects wryly on a failed sexual encounter but partly attributes his lack of success to the woman. Behn's poem instead portrays the male member as comically inadequate. Lysander's 'impatient Passion' overpowers Cloris, who responds with increasing enthusiasm to his overtures. At the moment of climax, however, Lysander suffers impotence ('Excess of Love his Love betray'd') and despite attempts to redeem the situation, 'The Insensible fell weeping in his Hand' (Behn 1992: 67). Cloris is left to muse on 'that Fabulous Priapus,/ That Potent God, as Poet's feign' (*ibid.*: 68): the rhetoric of male desire is far removed from its physical reality. By contrast, 'The Golden Age. A Paraphrase on a Translation out of French' (1684) envisions an ideal realm in which female desire and autonomy are celebrated: in this poem, sexuality is innocent, and free from the violence and dire social consequences that women experienced in Behn's age.

Elizabeth Barrett Browning draws on the friendship poem tradition in 'To George Sand: A Desire' (1844). The sonnet idealises the

French writer who, as 'large-brained woman and large-hearted man', challenges prevailing gender codes. Sand acquires quasi-divine status:

> I would some mild miraculous thunder ran
> Above the applauded circus, in appliance
> Of thine own nobler nature's strength and science –
> Drawing two pinions, white as wings of swan,
> From thy strong shoulders, to amaze the place
> With holier light! That thou to woman's claim,
> And man's might join beside the angel's grace
> Of a pure genius sanctified from blame;
> Till child and maiden pressed to thine embrace,
> To kiss upon thy lips a stainless fame.
> (Barrett Browning 1995: 320)

This passionate identification is intellectual and artistic, but the stress on physicality also implies a sublimated erotic element. Her *Sonnets from the Portuguese* (1846) follows the daunting tradition established by Petrarch, Sidney, Spenser and Shakespeare. In keeping with these forerunners, the sonnets establish a dialogue with the Beloved; although the rhetoric is overtly spiritual, however, the stress is on earthly love free from the power play of the courtly or seduction poem. Sonnet XXII restrains its own figurative momentum, and rejects an ascent to the angelic realm:

> When our two souls stand up erect and strong,
> Face to face, silent, drawing nigh & nigher,
> Until their lengthening wings break into fire
> At either curved point ... what bitter wrong,
> Can the earth do to us, that we should not long
> Be here contented?
> *(ibid.: 387)*

In the twentieth century, the conventions of love poetry are often treated sceptically. Larkin's 'High Windows' (Larkin 1988: 165) or 'Talking in Bed' (*ibid.*: 129) describe a failure of intimacy and reciprocity in emotional relationships amid the shallowness, anonymity and inauthenticity of a late modern society. The speaker's upward gaze in 'High Windows' implies a transcendent vision, but it can equally be interpreted as an aversion to 'kids' below: are the eyes cast heavenward in hope or despair? Carol Ann Duffy's recent collection, *Rapture*, articulates the power of sexual and emotional love, but 'The Love Poem' (Duffy 2005: 58) highlights the self-consciousness of the genre. The text is a tissue of quotations from love poems by Wyatt, Shakespeare, Barrett Browning and others, and 'love's lips' are indeed 'pursed to quotation marks'. This is a love poem addressed to itself, a hymn of praise, or a frustration with how lyric conventions stylise and exhaust passion. Contemporary popular music still draws on the thematics and modes of address associated with the love lyric: the urgent seduction of the rock song and the plangent, self-abasing appeal of the ballad have been staple features since the 1950s. (The latter has been given a fresh impetus by the 'boy band' phenomenon.) Here, too, the tension between spontaneous and formulaic utterance remains.

ELEGY AND LYRIC

In ancient Greece, elegies were accompanied by the flute, and their subject matter ranged from martial epigrams, philosophy and politics, to commemorations, amatory complaints, as well as funereal verse. Donne's *Elegies*, probably composed in the 1590s, followed the example of Ovid and other Roman poets in dealing with love rather than death, and love poetry and elegy have remained closely linked in the history of lyric. Elegy became identified as a genre dealing primarily with grief, loss, mourning and consolation in the modern period, and by the nineteenth century it was designated 'lyric' (Fowler 1982: 136–37). Elegy and lyric are connected by a concern with address, and the element of self-dramatisation. Peter Sacks argues that almost all elegies 'begin and continue in the mode of address' whereby 'the act of address invents the presence of an addressee' (Sacks 1985: 170). This is similar to love poetry, in that the focus rests on the speaker, the expression of feeling and depth of reflection, rather than on the object or figure addressed. In *Table Talk*, Coleridge ascribes to elegy the personal and introspective qualities typically associated with lyric: 'Elegy is the form of poetry natural to the reflective mind. It may treat of any subject, but it must treat of no subject for itself, but always and exclusively with reference to the poet himself' (cited by Lindley 1985: 68). This interiority and self-awareness is also characteristic of the love poem, which often serves to advertise the poet's credentials.

In the sixteenth and seventeenth centuries, the elegy can alternate between striking directness and intimacy and an elevated, public mode of address. Chidiock Tichborne's 'Elegy, Written in the Tower before his Execution' (1586) consigns itself to posterity, at once acknowledging and arresting the speaker's mortality:

> My prime of youth is but a frost of cares;
> My feast of joy is but a dish of pain;
> My crop of corn is but a field of tares;
> And all my good is but vain hope of gain:
> The day is past, and yet I saw no sun;
> And now I live, and now my life is done.
>
> My tale was heard, and yet it was not told;
> My fruit is fall'n, and yet my leaves are green;
> My youth is spent, and yet I am not old;
> I saw the world, and yet I was not seen:
> My thread is cut, and yet it is not spun;
> And now I live, and now my life is done.
>
> I sought for death, and found it in my womb;
> I looked for life, and saw it was a shade;
> I trod the earth, and knew it was my tomb;
> And now I die, and now I was but made:
> My glass is full, and now my glass is run;
> And now I live, and now my life is done.
>
> (Ault 1949: 120–21)

Ben Jonson's 'On My First Sonne' (1616) recounts a devastating bereavement, but in its apostrophe to the child the poem/ speaker is also concerned to ensure its survival:

Rest in soft peace, and, ask'd, say here doth lye
Ben. Ionson his best piece of *poetrie*.
For whose sake, hence-forth, all his vowes be such,
As what he loves may never like too much.
(Ricks 1999: 119)

In striking contrast, Katherine Philips's 'On the Death of My First and Dearest Child, Hector Philips' (1655) appears to lament its aesthetic failure in the face of death: 'Tears are my muse, and sorrow all my art,/ So piercing groans must be thy elegy.' Nevertheless the poem still bequeaths itself to the future:

An off'ring too for thy sad tomb I have,
Too just a tribute to thy early hearse.
Receive these gasping numbers to thy grave,
The last of thy unhappy mother's verse.
(Philips 1990: 220)

These poetic testaments illustrate Sacks's comment that most elegies attempt to keep the dead 'at some cleared distance from the living' (Sacks 1985: 19) Only survivors can 'do' elegy, and the dead, or the lost object of desire, must be separated from the poet by a veil of words (*ibid.*: 9).

These elegiac lyrics differ in scale and tone from the pastoral elegy and odes that commemorate the dead. In Milton's 'Lycidas' (1637), desire for the dead friend, and the accompanying pain of loss, is channelled into 'spiritual elevation' (*ibid.*: 94). Thomas Gray's 'Elegy on a Country Churchyard' (1742–50) mourns the anticipated death of the poet himself, and tries to ensure the survival of his voice. Shelley's 'Adonais' (1821) elevates the speaker, since the immortalised Keats is cast in Shelley's 'own ideal likeness' (*ibid.*: 159). The quiet, spiritual conviction of Tennyson's elegiac 'Crossing the Bar' (1889) does not lessen the metaphorical weight of its anticipated journey into the dark: the 'personal' meditation becomes a statement for posterity. This is underscored by Tennyson's insistence that the poem, not his last, should appear as the final poem in collections of his work.

Thomas Hardy's 1912–13 poems mark a return to the lyric of personal loss, and their apostrophes lack the conviction and self-aggrandizing elements of the 'public' elegy. In 'The Walk' (Hardy 1923: 320), the speaker is 'undone' (Sacks 1985: 245) by the way the vacant room returns his gaze: 'familiar ground' is surveyed once more, but the absence of the 'you' produces an 'underlying sense' of difference. In 'The Voice' (Hardy 1923: 325), the 'woman much missed' calls to the speaker, but the uncertainty of whether it is 'you that I hear' implies that is merely a fading echo of the speaker's own voice or the 'breeze' rather than a ghostly plea. The poem ends with the speaker 'faltering forward' but still hearing the woman's call across a wintry landscape.

While two world wars prompted many elegiac lyrics, including Wilfred Owen's 'Anthem for Doomed Youth', Jahan Ramazani has argued that the twentieth-century elegy has flourished through being anti-elegiac in form and sceptical about its consolatory possibilities (Ramazani 1994: xi). W. H. Auden's elegies for Yeats and Freud, and his 'Stop the Clocks' (made famous by its use in the film *Four Weddings and a Funeral*), are marked by casual disregard for generic conventions and a conversational manner. In recent years, Douglas Dunn's *Elegies* (1985), and Seamus Heaney's *Field Work* (1979) and *Station Island* (1984), have charted loss in lyric sequences that adopt a 'private' rather than 'public' register. Geoffrey Hill's 'September Song' (Hill 1986: 67) remains one of the most powerful elegiac lyrics of the post-war period. Its commemoration of the victims of the Holocaust is characterised by terse understatement – the 14 elliptical lines are 'more than enough' – but is also marked by ethical hesitation about the aestheticisation of such suffering. While the overtly sacralising element is often absent in the modern elegiac lyric, its self-conscious construction of a poetic voice continues to be central.

American elegies in the modern period, such as Walt Whitman's 'When Lilacs Last in the Dooryard Bloom'd' (addressed to Abraham Lincoln), Allen Tate's 'Ode to the Confederate Dead' and Robert Lowell's 'For the Union Dead', are often more explicitly public, and are also overtly concerned with the loss of paternal authority. In these poems of occasion, the mourners tend to be outsiders (Sacks 1985: 313), thus fitting the conventional mould of the post-Romantic lyric speaker. Plath's 'Daddy' is a partial exception to this pattern. The speaker is ambiguously positioned in relation to the lost father, and the attitude is ambivalent. This uncertainty is underscored by the poem's oscillation between the love lyric and elegy. It parodies the Petrarchan blazon, which divides the woman's body into separate parts in order to praise their beauty, by itemising the father's eye, chin, head, heart and foot. This suggests that the father is an idealised, inaccessible figure akin to the Lady of the courtly poem, but the dialogue between 'I' and the 'you' is violently confrontational. While the apostrophic address attempts to sever connections and push the father into oblivion, the declaration 'I'm through' does not provide convincing closure. It can be read as settling final accounts with the father, but equally implies that the daughter wishes to be reunited with him. The father's legacy remains to be negotiated, and this family drama is without resolution in the present time of the text.

Amy Clampitt's 'Procession at Candlemas' attempts to refeminise the elegy, but a more striking challenge to male tradition is offered by Gwendolyn Brooks's 'the mother' (Rees-Jones 2005: 103). The structure of address shifts disconcertingly in the poem. The voice in the first stanza is a generalised 'you' ('Abortions will not let you forget'), then moves to a first person 'I' that assumes maternal responsibility for all of the deaths in the poem. This intimacy is produced by the wind, which carries the voices of the dead children to the speaker's ear. The invocation of the wind recalls Shelley's 'Ode to the West Wind', but whereas in Shelley this invisible force is an animating spirit that breathes power into the poet, in Brooks it brings guilt, responsibility, and a failure of language: 'what shall I say, how is the truth to be said?'. Thus Brooks explicitly rewrites a male lyric tradition, 'textually placing aborted children in the spot formerly occupied by the dead, inanimate, or absent entities previously addressed by the lyric tradition' (Johnson, Barbara 1991: 634). Does the poem accuse the 'mother' of murder, given that the apostrophe humanises the children? Or does its struggle with articulation to express her pain and acute loss? Like the love poem, the elegy is a question of gender and sexual politics.

DEVOTIONAL LYRICS

Chapter 3 demonstrated that sacred and secular lyrics can be seen as 'generic twins' (Lindley 1985: 8). Helen Vendler argues that, while lyric may exist in the 'here and now', it also exists nowhere: 'the lyric is the gesture of immortality and freedom: the novel is the gesture of the historical and spatial' (cited by Cook 2004: 577). This makes explicit the quasi-spiritual connotations of lyric. To some extent, Vendler underscores Adorno's account of the lyric in terms of utopian yearning, although from a very different theoretical and political standpoint. Abrams points out that the high valuation of lyric forms in Western culture derived in part from the view that Biblical poetry, especially the Psalms of David, was lyric in character (Abrams 1953: 86). The Bible contained not only secular lyrics (songs of work, drinking, war) and spiritual lyrics (hymns and laments), but also didactic and instructive forms (riddles, proverbs, parables) that featured in worldly and religious poetry from the early Christian through to the modern period. This explains Tzvetan Todorov's contention that 'certain instances of lyric poetry and prayer have more rules in common than that same poetry and the historical novel of the *War and Peace* variety' (Todorov 1990: 11).

During the medieval and early modern periods, the erotic and spiritual, the devotional song and the love lyric are often intertwined. In medieval lyrics, the Virgin Mary could become the courtly mistress, while the neoplatonism that informs the courtly love poem celebrates physical passion while also recognising 'the beloved as a reflection of the divine' (Cohen 1963: 52). The symbolic meaning of the Corpus Christi Carol from the sixteenth century (Davies 1963: 363–64) is conventionally Christian in its references to the Eucharist and the Grail, but it may also allude to Anne Boleyn, whose badge was the falcon. Thus the text carries a political and sexual charge, alongside its ostensible religious purpose. In the seventeenth century, the tension between conviction and doubt, verbal violence and the dramatised self are common to both Donne's amorous and religious poetry. Donald Davie notes the influence of Horace's *carmina* on hymn-writers in the eighteenth century, such as Isaac Watts and Charles Wesley (Davie

1974: 6). The 'I' of the hymn also resembles the courtly lover, an unworthy supplicant who seeks the favour of a transcendent other. The self-abasing speaker of Watts's 'Crucifixion to the World by the Cross of Christ' surrenders to an all-consuming, divine love:

> When I survey the wond'rous Cross
> Where the young Prince of Glory dy'd,
> My richest Gain I count but Loss,
> And pour Contempt on all my Pride.
> [...]
> Were the whole Realm of Nature mine,
> That were a present far too small;
> Love so amazing, so divine
> Demand my Soul, my Life, my All.
>
> (Davie 1974: 51)

This appeal is replicated in Augustus Toplady's 'A Living and Dying Prayer for the Holiest Believer in the World':

> Nothing in my Hand I bring;
> Simply to thy Cross I cling;
> Naked, come to Thee for Dress;
> Helpless, look to Thee for Grace;
> Foul, I to the Fountain fly:
> Wash me, Saviour, or I die!
>
> (*ibid.*: 105).

The hymn foregrounds the speaker/singer's nakedness and vulnerability: only in a realm beyond the mortal will the self find refuge and succour. Similarly to the love lyric, this hymn is at once a profession of faith and humility, and an exercise in persuasion. There is also a more prosaic dimension to the hymn's concern with indebtedness and worthiness. Davie explains that the text first appeared in the *Gospel Magazine* in 1776, 'where it is the climax of an extraordinary catechism which, beginning with computations to show the impossibility of paying off the National Debt, goes on to compute the impossibility of man's paying off his debt to God, supposing that he sins every second of his life' (*ibid.*: 166). The commercial logic that underpins Protestant doctrine here – the worldly measure of unworldly desire – is perhaps the equivalent of the courtly lyric 200 years previously, where extravagant declarations and idealisations of love and virtue were often indirect appeals for patronage and advancement.

In the early modern period, Protestantism mutes the collective experience associated with medieval devotional verse. Gary Waller notes the similarities between the Petrarchan and the Protestant self: each is self-obsessed, preoccupied with transience and the fleeting pleasures and limitations of earthly love (Waller 1993: 97). The courtly lyric was influenced by the Protestant emphasis on meditation, soliloquy and self-scrutiny (Lewalski 1979: 171), while the refinement of poetic style and diction in Petrarchan lyric suited English religious lyric, since it represented a reaction to the perceived vulgarity and vacuity of love poetry (Peterson 1967: 175). Protestant devotional verse also drew on biblical poetic forms (psalms, hymns and songs) that replicated many of the main functions of secular lyric: meditation, praise and celebration. Ramie Targoff remarks that by the early seventeenth century, 'the act of writing a poem and rendering it skillfully in rhyme' became 'its own form of prayer' (Targoff 2001: 84).

Most poets in the seventeenth century produced religious poetry, and it is artificial to separate spiritual and secular lyrics in a period marked by religious and political schism, and in which public profession and private faith intersected so strongly (Parfitt 1992: 62). This religious poetry takes very different forms: while Henry Vaughan and Richard Crashaw stress the visionary and transcendental elements of faith (Parfitt 1992: 59), Donne's lyrics evoke an intimate relationship to God, but it is one that involves struggle and self-interrogation. His religious poetry can be described as 'spiritual autobiography', and has little sense of the 'congregational', or 'the poet-figure as representative of or part of the community' (*ibid.*: 50). While the congregational aspect is more pronounced in the work of George Herbert, one of the most prominent religious lyric poets of the century, there is still a preoccupation with poetic subjectivity. In *The Temple* (1633), Herbert applies 'the skill and introspection that we traditionally associate with private meditations or erotic sonnets to poems that seem designed to be shared with others' (Targoff 2001: 103). Herbert's 'The Flower', for example, negotiates between a subjective and intersubjective voice. Its account of individual spiritual crisis is resolved by the renewal of poetic creativity:

> And now in age I bud again,
> After so many deaths I live and write;
> I once more smell the dew and rain,
> And relish versing. Oh, my only light,
> It cannot be
> That I am he
> On whom thy tempests fell all night.
> (Abrams 1993: 1384–85)

The speaker's 'recovered greenness' does not lead to self-absorption, and the poem instead assumes a collective devotional experience (Targoff 2001: 99) by switching from 'I' to 'we':

> These are thy wonders, Lord of love,
> To make us see we are but flowers that glide;
> Which when we once can find and prove
> Thou hast a garden for us where to bide.
> (Abrams 1993: 1384–85)

The poem certainly reflects on the trials of writing, but it is equally about the trials of faith, and the relationship of the 'I' to God and the world. In the later twentieth century, R. S. Thomas's 'The Moor' (Thomas 1994: 88) rehearses this natural renewal of poetry and faith. It owes a debt to the topographical poem, but resists the greater lyric's urge to colonise the scene. The moor is 'like' a church, but the God that is present is 'felt' rather than 'listened to'. In this epiphanic moment, the speaker's mind cedes its 'kingdom' and, like Herbert, Thomas relinquishes the overweening lyric voice.

Romantic poetry constitutes a secular reinvigoration of lyric's religious functions, and at times becomes 'theological in expression' (Abrams 1965: 555), yet it privileges a personal rather than communal spiritual experience. Shelley's statement in 'A Defence of Poetry' that 'poetry is indeed something divine' positions itself against Peacock's observation in *The Four Ages of Poetry* that poetry 'takes its rise in the demand for the commodity, and flourishes in proportion to the extent of the market' (cited by Lindley 1985: 69). The elevated yearning for prophetic or transcendent experience in the greater ode may be loosely likened to a hymn, but Gene W. Ruoff has stressed its difference from more conventional spiritual discourse:

> Hymns are to be sung by congregations as acts of devotion; whatever their archaic communal origins, odes have in modern practice become monodies, or if they contain multiple voices, those voices as frequently clash as harmonize, and any ultimate harmonies they express must be won rather than presupposed.
>
> (Ruoff 1989: 195)

Shelley's nightingale poet is an elevated but isolated being whose rapturous melody cannot mute an uncertainty regarding the function and value of poetry. John Creaser comments that, despite their 'eager greeting of objects of veneration', Romantic odes 'are elegiac and nostalgic in feeling. They speak of a state of wholeness and old certainties out of a conviction of loss' (Creaser 1998: 243). In contrast, William Blake's poetry is explicitly spiritual, deploying the proverbs and folk rhymes that are common in the Bible. John Holloway has traced the continuity between Blake's lyrics and the hymns of his time. *Songs of Innocence* has the homiletic quality of medieval religious verse, and their apparent childlike spontaneity has an educative purpose. Holloway also shows how 'The Tyger' sustains, but also challenges, the hymn tradition of the eighteenth century (Holloway 1968: 47). Blake, like other Romantic poets, invests the lyric with prophetic power, but he draws on a religious tradition that depersonalises the 'I'.

Barrett Browning's *Sonnets from the Portuguese* negotiate between this depersonalised, collective voice of devotional verse and the ardent supplicant of the courtly lyric. Sonnet XLII interweaves erotic and spiritual longing, and submits secular love to divine sanction:

> How do I love thee? Let me count the ways! –
> I love thee to the depth &breadth & height
> My soul can reach, when feeling out of sight
> For the ends of Being and Ideal Grace.
> I love thee to the level of everyday's
> Most quiet need, by sun & candlelight –
> I love thee freely, as men strive for Right, –
> I love thee purely, as they turn from Praise;
> I love thee with the passion, put to use
> In my old griefs, ... and with my childhood's faith.
> I love thee with the love I seemed to lose
> With my lost Saints, – I love thee with the breath,
> Smiles, tears, of all my life! – and, if God choose,
> I shall but love thee better after my death.
>
> (Barrett Browning 1995: 398)

The sonnet is an emotional and intellectual exercise that combines the passion for the unattainable beloved, the hymn of spiritual praise, and the elegiac meditation that commits itself to posterity. It reaches beyond the self, language, religious doubt and mortality, driven by the desire that connects these different forms of lyric.

6

LYRIC, MUSIC AND PERFORMANCE

In the early modern period, the development of print culture fundamentally altered the relationship between music and poetry, and the link grew progressively more vestigial. While the nature of this ancient connection between words and song may remain inaccessible to us in its original Greek form (Johnson 1982: 26–27), it can still be discerned in the often vaguely applied adjective 'lyrical' (Lindley 1985: 23–24). Lyrics designed to be sung or recited produce different effects from a 'private' reading of poetry on the page, but enduring links between lyric and music can be traced through, for example, the Provençal troubadour tradition, popular ballads, the rich combination of music and text in the Elizabethan period, the hymn tradition from the seventeenth century onwards, the folk songs of Woody Guthrie, Pete and Peggy Seeger, Ewan MacColl and Bob Dylan, and in the resurgence of performance poetry that is tied to various musical traditions in the later twentieth century. This chapter considers the residual connections between poetry and musical performance in the history of lyric. It shows that poetry and music have been combined for overtly politicised, as well as celebratory, purposes in both 'high' and popular culture. In doing so, it illustrates a central theme of this book: rather than presenting the spontaneous feelings of a private individual, lyric is a self-conscious form of address that must negotiate with a world beyond the self.

BABBLE AND DOODLE

Northrop Frye has defined the two boundaries of lyric as the musical ('*melos*') and the pictorial ('*opsis*'), and the primordial forms of these poles are 'babble' and 'doodle' (Frye 1957: 275). Babble concerns rhythm, and at its most fundamental it features in chants, nursery rhymes, lullabies and incantations. Doodle is a matter of verbal and conceptual design, visible in the numerous verse forms associated with lyric. Discussions about the relationship between lyric and music have tended to revolve around these poles. Blake's 'The Tyger' illustrates the interdependence of *melos* and *opsis* in lyric practice, challenging the view that '[t]he essential beauty of a lyric lies in the melody of the oral word – sung, intoned or spoken; it has nothing whatever to do with the orthography of the written word' (Ault 1949: xiii). The poem is a mixture of nursery rhyme rhythm, incantation and hymn, but it also draws on Blake's knowledge of the emblematic tradition (Welsh 1978: 9).

Yet the conventions of lyric, rooted in the ancient association between lyric and music and the 'oral' fiction discussed in Chapter 2, tend to 'ask us to respond to poetry on the level of sound rather than content and as song rather than language' (Rajan 1985: 199). Neil Corcoran has recently remarked that a lyric poem 'is always also a musical score of a kind, a set of instructions for the production of sound' (Corcoran 2002: 10). This demonstrates that the theory and practice of lyric in the twentieth and twenty-first centuries remain strongly attached to the aural properties of lyric. In the early twentieth century, William Carlos Williams declared that 'by its *music* shall the best of modern verse be known and the *resources* of its music' (cited by Scully 1966: 71). The Imagist movement identified *melos* as one of its three foundational principles in 1913: 'As regarding rhythm: to compose in sequence of the musical phrase, not in sequence of the metronome' (Jones 1972: 129). A year later, Ezra Pound defined lyric as 'a sort of poetry where music, sheer melody, seems as if it were just bursting into speech' (cited by Jones 1972: 21). Pound identified the *melopoeia* of lyric poetry with musical composition, conversational speech and incantation, a demonstration that post-Romantic theories of lyric have continued to preserve 'that archaic sense of casting a spell, or magical compulsion, that comes to it from charm' (Welsh 1978: 148). Frye argues that the free verse experimentation of modern lyric poetry 'liberated' the distinctive music of lyric, inherited from its ancient link with chant, song and ritual performance: 'an oracular, meditative, irregular, unpredictable, and essentially discontinuous rhythm, emerging from the coincidences of the sound-pattern' (Frye 1957: 271). Eliot's 'Rhapsody on a Windy Night', with its incantatory repetitions, irregular rhythms, non-linearity and startling imagery, epitomises this return to the 'primitive'.

For all this perceived primitive musicality, and the musical structure of *Four Quartets*, however, Eliot declared that it is only 'in dramatic verse in its greatest intensity' that we approach the condition of music. Anything other than this tentative proximity would 'annihilate' poetry (Eliot 1990: 86–87). Two anthologies of lyric in the later twentieth century offer strikingly different views of its relationship to music. C. Day Lewis's *English Lyric Poems 1500–1900* (1961) stresses the anonymous or communal voice of ballads and folk songs. Lyric is predominantly poetry meant to be sung, and is closely related to story-telling: two of the four sections of the Anthology are entitled 'Songs' and 'Story-Lyrics', while 'Lyrical Poems' and 'Devotional Lyrics' deal with meditative, 'personal' poems. The refrain is posited as central to lyric: 'One could almost define the song lyric as a poem in which, even when there is not verbal refrain, the ear is made to expect one' (Day Lewis 1961: 6). The open-endedness of refrain, which gives a great deal of scope for additions and variations, compares favourably with the closure of narrative forms (Jeffreys 1995: 201). Contrastingly, Elder Olson's *American Lyric Poems: From Colonial Times to the Present* (1964) rejects the link between lyric and song: 'what has musical accompaniment to do with literary form? Almost anything can be set to music for a particular instrument; in any case, that seems a composer's concern, not a poet's' (Olson 1964: 1). Given that Olson does not include American folk songs, work songs or spirituals, his editorial judgement is not only formalist, but implicitly political.

David Lindley has attempted to circumvent essentialising accounts of lyric and music by providing a series of descriptive categories. Lindley first distinguishes words written to be set to music and written poems that were subsequently set to music. In practice, these distinctions are often hard to draw, since many poets in the early modern period, such as Thomas Campion, were also composers, and twentieth-century songwriters such as Cole Porter, Noel Coward, Bob Dylan, Joni Mitchell and Leonard Cohen composed words and music simultaneously. Lindley then separates lyrics destined to be set to music and those that 'declare an affiliation with the forms and conventions of song' (Lindley 1985: 27). Music can feature as a thematic concern in, for example, Coleridge's 'The Eolian Harp' or Barrett Browning's 'A Musical Instrument' (1860). Alternatively, musical forms and rhythms may be incorporated into the lyric poem. The song-like quality of Hardy's 'The Voice' is accentuated by its triple dance rhythm, which allegedly derives from 'Haste to the Wedding', one of Hardy's and his late wife Emma's favourite songs as a young couple (Brooks 1971: 83). The alternating masculine and feminine end-rhymes, moving from a rising to a dying cadence, takes the poem from its song-like opening to a hesitant, unmelodic, stumbling conclusion that offers 'a halting expression of utter loss' (Sacks 1985: 248).

Lindley also locates a major shift in the perception of the relationship between lyric and music in the late eighteenth century, when German aesthetic tradition elevated music above poetry as an expressive art. According to Schlegel, lyric poetry, unlike music, was dependent on an external object 'for the expression of feeling' (Abrams 1953: 93–94). From this point, lyrics become poems that work in ways analogous to music, and music becomes a way of describing the purpose of poetry. This has major consequences for lyric: 'From being poetry that organizes language so that it may be accommodated to musical setting, lyric becomes language so disposed that it imitates music in effect' (Lindley 1985: 30). In light of this transformation, Lindley concentrates on the aspects of formal organisation that link lyric and music, particularly 'features of repetition' such as the refrain, rhyme and rhythm (*ibid*.: 31).

This chapter approaches the relationship between lyric and music from a different perspective. Rather than pursuing a formalist approach in order to classify the 'musical' qualities of lyric, it shows how relationships between song and the written word are intimately tied to shifting historical circumstances. Again, Blake's 'The Tyger' is instructive. As Chapter 5 noted, the poem draws on didactic verse forms, as well as on the hymn tradition of the eighteenth century, in order to question religious orthodoxy. Blake deploys modes that are closely tied to popular culture and music, and eschews the meditative, interior lyric. Blake's poetic strategy reveals a recurrent feature of lyric: its role can be epideictic and tied to the interests of power, but it can also be harnessed for the purposes of critique and dissent.

SONG AND DANCE: LYRIC AND POPULAR CULTURE

W. R. Johnson comments, that in Greek lyric, 'music existed for the sake of the words'. The performance of the poem, and the intelligibility of the song's words, was what mattered: music intensified the words, rather than decorated them (Johnson 1982: 27–28). The narrative emphasis of Greek heroic epic was also driven by the demands of musical performance: the formulaic phrases of Homeric poetry would have functioned as mnemonic devices for the performer, and would also have provided an anchoring point for the audience. The bardic tradition persisted in predominantly oral cultures until the early medieval in England, and remained a strong feature of Celtic cultures in Ireland, Scotland and Wales into the modern period. The Anglo-Saxon *scop* performed elegies and retold ancient legends to the accompaniment of a harp. The lyre found in the seventh-century royal ship burial at Sutton Hoo indicates the importance accorded to poetic song in Anglo-Saxon culture (Bradley 1982: xv). The poet in medieval Europe could sing unaccompanied or accompanied by a harp or a lute, or could be joined by another musician, who would play bowed instruments such as the rebec or the viol. Both respectable minstrels and strolling players were, in modern parlance, touring singer–songwriters. Some might receive regular patronage as semi-permanent members of a court, or episcopal and aristocratic households, while others would travel between courts, carrying letters of recommendations from their patrons.

Thus the 'high' lyric mode is linked inextricably to the medieval ballad due to its primarily oral character. The ballad has conventionally been treated as a formulaic poetic mode, reliant on dialogue, narrative and repeated phrases, making it seem far distant from the rhapsodic lyric (Bold 1979). Albert Lord has argued that, unlike the literary poem, there is no original moment of composition for the oral ballad:

> For the oral poet, the moment of composition is the performance. In the case of a literary poem there is a gap in time between the composition and reading or performance; in the case of the oral poem this gap does not exist, because composition and performance are two aspects of the same moment.
>
> (Lord 1960: 13)

Yet several objections can be raised to this decisive separation of oral and literary lyric. Ruth Finnegan cites Eskimo and Gaelic court poetry as cases in which the creation of oral poetry 'is due to long deliberation before the performance' (Finnegan 1977: 80), thus qualifying its degree of spontaneity. Finnegan points out that both oral poetry and lyric encompass great generic range and diversity, from love songs, praise and hymns to laments and lullabies (*ibid.*: 13). Antony Easthope also objects to Lord's theory by emphasising that each reading of a written poem is in part context-specific, and is remade each time it is performed (Easthope 1983: 80). In addition, we have seen how the structure of address within lyric poem is invariably performative, at once positioning and demanding a response of its addressee. The fact that ballads have been transcribed and recorded for many centuries, and lyric poems have been set to music, further blurs the oral/written distinction.

The anonymous medieval ballad 'The Three Ravens', first printed in 1611, illustrates this intermingling of oral and literary forms:

There were three ravens sat on a tree,
Down a down, hay down, hay down,
There were three ravens sat on a tree,
With a down,
There were three ravens sat on a tree,
They were as black as they might be,
With a down, derry, derry, derry, down, down.
The one of them said to his mate,
'Where shall we our breakfast take?'
'Down in yonder green field
There lies a knight slain under his shield.
His hounds they lie down at this feet,
So well they can their master keep.'
'His hawks they fly so eagerly,
There's no fowl dare him come nigh.'
Down there comes a fallow doe,
As great with young as she might go.
She lifted up his bloody head,
And kissed his wounds that were so red.
She got him up upon her back,
And carried him to earthen lake.
She buried him before the prime;
She was dead herself ere evensong time.
God send every gentleman
Such hawks, such hounds, and such a lemman.

(Abrams 1993: 392–93)

The poem follows the pattern of the repetition of the first line and the refrains. The refrain, colloquial vocabulary and uncluttered syntax indicate the text's musical origins, and the repeated 'down' may suggest a dance movement. These communal features are underscored by the intersubjective point of view: the solitary lyric 'I' is absent. The ballad combines several different lyric forms – the lament, the love song and the devotional poem – and didactic and narrative elements are also prominent. It displays many of the trappings of the courtly poem – the lord, his hounds and the deer – and appears to perform an epideictic function by idealising feudal relations. Yet the point of view is uncertain: the poem may endorse the superiority of the knight, but its sympathy may equally lie with the ravens. In life, the knight's wealth and power were symbolised by the hounds and hawks; in death, they protect his body from scavengers. Whether the poem is read as serving the interests of power, or as articulating dissent, the lyric/ballad mode engages with its social world. In contrast to the modern lyric, the addressee of 'The Three Ravens' is offered only a relative position (Easthope 1983: 93), and the act of interpretation is dependent on the context of the poem's performance and reception.

The ability of lyric to serve 'high' and popular culture in the medieval and early modern periods was mirrored by musical composition. There was a recurrent concern stretching into the modern period about the decline of sacred, serious music into the profanity of popular song. In practice, however, music and poetry devoted to sacred and secular music were closely interwoven, and sequences of religious music could freely borrow melodies from earlier popular songs. Peter Dronke reminds us that '[o]ne of the prime functions of lyric throughout the Middle Ages was to accompany dancing' (Dronke 1968: 186), and dance songs formed a central part of religious worship and secular festivals. Dance songs such as the carol and *rondeau* could have complex musical arrangements and choreography, with a simpler refrain to enable audience participation. Medieval dance could also be used to symbolise the harmony of the heavens or the cycles of life and death. *Carmina Burana*, a mixture of Latin and vernacular German, blends Christian and pagan rituals and meanings, and its central figure is a ring of dancers. '*Sumer is icumen in*', a staple of English folk song tradition that celebrates fertility and the cycle of the seasons, also had its origins in pre-Christian and secular festivals.

The Elizabethan period has been regarded as a golden age of 'musical' lyric. W. B. Sedgwick casts the Elizabethan lyric in the spirit of its Greek original, declaring that 'even in the slightest of these poems we are apt to find with a thrill the most surprising verbal harmony, and that inevitableness of expression which we call the lyric cry: they are true lyrics; they are songs' (Sedgwick 1924: 101). In his 1949 anthology *Elizabethan Lyrics*, however, Norman Ault stresses the importance of seeing the Elizabethan lyric poem 'in relation to its proper historical background of contemporary song' (Ault 1949: v), and this historical context shapes the interaction of lyric poetry and music. At a time when verbal display, rhetorical skill and performance are paramount, music and poetry become complementary forms. While composers could set anonymous, popular lyrics – John Taverner's setting of 'Western Wind' is an example – the dominance of the courtly poem meant that much musical composition took on a more pronounced 'literary' character. In the period, songs, like poems, were subject to a generic hierarchy. The air, a song for the single voice, was regarded as a less weighty and learned verse form than the madrigal, which has several voices singing contrapuntally. The musical complexity of the madrigal, inherited from mainland Europe and developed by William Byrd, Orlando Gibbons and Thomas Morley, among others, is matched by its intricate verbal arrangements. As such, it is a markedly 'literary' musical form, and was deemed suitable for dealing with serious or passionate subjects (Ing 1951: 70). Morley composed songs for Shakespeare's *As You Like it* and *Twelfth Night*, while the dirge in Act 4, Scene 2 of *Cymbeline* ('Fear no more the heat o' the sun') might be regarded as exemplary of the song lyric (Hobsbaum 1996: 37). Music for dance and for song also had a daily role in the Jacobean and Caroline courts, and lyric poetry and print culture were closely related to non-print, performance forms outside the court, including theatre (Corns 1998: 55).

Yet John Stevens has suggested that the 'natural and necessary union of music and poetry' had already broken up in the fourteenth century (Stevens 1979: 35). Musical composition for secular and sacred purposes increasingly attempted to imitate human speech; Stevens points out that Tudor song-books between 1480–1530 copied not only the duration of speech syllables, but also 'the intonation of speech in musical melody' (*ibid.*: 102). Thus music increasingly operates as the support and ornamentation for words and meaning, a shift that is accentuated in the seventeenth century. The meditative intensity of John Dowland's songs compares with the lyrics of his contemporary, Donne. In the Caroline period, Henry Lawes, Gentleman of the Royal Chapel, set numerous poems by Carew, Herrick, Waller, Suckling and Lovelace, and his compositions, like those of Nicholas Lanier, Master of the King's Music, brought song closer to normal speech rhythms (Corns 1998: 55). This paralleled developments in poetic form, where rhythm and diction were increasingly influenced by plain rather than eloquent speech.

The eighteenth century revived the link between lyric and music. Donald Davie defines eighteenth-century lyric as 'a poem composed either to match an existing piece of music, or in the expectation and hope of a musical setting being contrived for it' (Davie 1974: 4). While there was a rich hymn-writing tradition in the period, lyric was also highly 'public' and politicised. Hymns on martial and patriotic themes that responded to con-temporary historical events were popular, and were tied, as in the previous century, to theatrical performances. Lyric takes on an epideictic role, and plays its part in the national story. James Thomson's 'Rule, Britannia' was composed for a masque com-missioned by the Prince of Wales in 1740 for the birthday of his eldest child. In the masque, the song celebrates the victory of King Alfred over the Danes. The refrain now resounds each year at the Last Night of the Proms, returning lyric verse to its com-munal and ceremonial origins. Henry Carey's 'A Loyal Song', subtitled 'Sung at the Theatres', became the National Anthem during the reign of George II. The hymn was probably composed in 1739, performed by the writer in 1740, and given its title in the aftermath of the failed Jacobite rebellion in 1745. The renowned actor David Garrick's famous 'Hearts of Oak' was composed for the pantomime *Harlequin's Invasion* in 1758, the year that Quebec fell to the British:

Come cheer up my lads, 'tis to glory we steer,
To add something new to this wonderful year.
To honour we call you, not press you like slaves,
For who are so free as the sons of the waves?
[Chorus]
Hearts of oak are our ships, hearts of oak are our men;
We always are ready – steady, boys, steady –
We'll fight and we'll conquer again and again.
                    (Brooks and Faulkner 1996: 86–87)

In contrast to these poems of celebration and commemoration, 'public' lyrics could also express political dissent. Cowper's 'The Negro's Complaint', written in 1788, is a strident attack on slavery, underpinned by strong religious conviction. It is composed 'To the tune of Hosiers Ghost', a reference to Richard Glover's 'Admiral Hosier's Ghost', which indirectly attacked the Prime Minister Sir Robert Walpole for failing to support the eponymous Admiral in his naval blockade of Spanish harbours in the West Indies in 1726. Cowper re-uses the tune to accompany his exposure of England's present shame in supporting and sustaining the slave trade. In the song, the dehumanised slave deploys his sophisticated voice and consciousness in order to condemn the inhumanity of a supposedly civilised nation. Cowper's song quickly became a rallying cry for abolitionists, and the first and last stanzas convey its rhetorical strategy:

> Forc'd from home, and all its pleasures,
> Afric's coast I left forlorn;
> To increase a stranger's treasures,
> O'er the raging billows borne.
> Men from England bought and sold me,
> Paid my price in paltry gold;
> But, though theirs they have enroll'd me,
> Minds are never to be sold.
> [...]
> Deem our nation brutes no longer
> Till some reason ye shall find
> Worthier of regard and stronger
> Than the colour of our kind.
> Slaves of gold, whose sordid dealings
> Tarnish all your boasted pow'rs,
> Prove that you have human feelings
> Ere you proudly question ours!
>
> (Davie 1974: 122).

The eighteenth century represents a watershed for lyric forms overtly tied to court culture, royal patronage and theatrical performance.

As we saw in Chapter 4, the Romantic period affirms its musical provenance by investing the voice with transcendental power, but also by reclaiming and reinventing the ballad and bardic traditions. Wordsworth's Preface to *Lyrical Ballads* is split between a view of lyric as lofty utterance and popular song, and individual and representative voice, oral and print culture. While Wordsworth affirms authentic culture and 'ordinary' speech, he converts 'the embedded narrative of social community into the transcendent lyric of a universal subject' (Janowitz 1998: 45). Anne Janowitz contrasts Wordsworth's view of the communal voice of lyric poetry with that of his contemporary, the radical London republican George Dyer. Two of Dyer's essays published in 1802, 'Lyric Poetry' and 'Representative Poetry', articulate 'his interest in the lyric as a literary form of cultural liberation' (*ibid*.: 52). In the first essay, Dyer challenges the hierarchical valuation of 'lofty' lyric:

> The tender ballad, the sprightly song, and even the humorous tale, possess the character of lyric poetry, no less than the compositions of higher pretension, as to subject, and of more magnificent appearance, as to structure.
>
> *(ibid.:* 53)

In the second essay, Dyer advocates a lyric mode that does not elevate the poet 'above his ordinary material self' and leave him 'confined by his own individuality'. The representative poet 'of necessity resigns his own individuality ... He ceases to be himself' (*ibid*.: 54–55). This recalls Keats's remarks on the 'egotistical sublime', but Wordsworth's version of a lyric 'I' apparently unbound by the constraints of time and space won out in critical and popular reception. For example, Robert Burns was vaunted by literary culture as the true voice of popular ballad – Coleridge anointed him 'Nature's own beloved bard' (Low 1974: 22) – but he was posthumously constructed as the typically isolated, marginalised Romantic poet. While the celebration of Burns's authenticity helped to mute the radical politics that underpinned the ballad tradition he represented, however, he became 'a powerful emblem of the congregating force of song' for radical movements in the nineteenth century (Janowitz 1998: 67).

This other voice – musical, communal – of Romantic lyric is audible in Wordsworth's 'The Solitary Reaper'. The 'melancholy strain' sung by the 'solitary Highland lass' may be a folk song in a Gaelic tongue suppressed by the Highland clearances. As such, it is a testament to an extreme form of the type of agrarian disruption and displacement visible in the Lakeland rural culture evoked in *Lyrical Ballads*. Similarly to Keats's 'Ode to a Nightingale', the speaker cannot hear or comprehend the song. Although it is imaginatively appropriated ('The music in my heart I bore/ Long after it was heard no more') its remote, enigmatic force remains as a challenge to the poet's creative supremacy. More obliquely, the ballad tetrameter and narrative emphasis of Blake's 'London' also provides a counterpoint to Wordsworth's sonnet 'Composed upon Westminster Bridge, September 3, 1802'. The rhetorical and metrical momentum of Blake's poem conveys the movement and clamour of the city streets: the alternating iambic and trochaic feet, and the use of anaphora, orchestrate the prophetic urgency of its appeal. In contrast, Wordsworth's stately, regular pentameter, the artificially naturalised rhythm of English verse, complements the detachment of the speaker and the tranquillity of the idealised city in the poet's post-revolutionary years. The pun on 'still' in the final line carefully balances change and stasis: London's heart continues to beat, but in this lyric interlude it pauses, as if outside the passage of time. Blake's poem demands action; Wordsworth's resists it.

While the sense of lyric as song-like has receded in poetic theory and practice in the past two centuries, the residual connection between words and music has survived in a range of forms such as folk song, blues, dub poetry and rap. In recent years, interest in lyric as performance has also revived. The links between poetry and popular music can be traced in a number of directions. In the 1950s and 1960s, the work of the Beats and the Mersey poets was interwoven with popular music and public, often counter-cultural, performance. The Scottish poet, singer–songwriter, storyteller and epigrammatist Ivor Cutler, whose performance style and often surreal humour were as distinctive as his lyrics, appeared in the 1967 Beatles film, *Magical Mystery Tour*, and he also recorded albums of his songs. Debates about the literary merits of pop songs have long grown sterile, but Andrew Ross cautions against the 'formalistic analysis' of lyrics:

> In many cases, we mishear the lyrics of pop songs, and when we do hear them correctly, we usually listen selectively, since our attention is more engaged with the 'sound' of the lyrics, interacting with the music, rather than with the meaning of the words themselves.
>
> (Ross 1991: 98)

The 'interiority' of singer–songwriters such as Bob Dylan, Joni Mitchell and Leonard Cohen fit the conventional poetic mould more obviously, and these figures self-consciously reproduce many of the typical features associated with lyric. Their carefully crafted songs pay meticulous attention to rhythm and stress, and convey a story or situation within strict time limitations. Cohen has published his writing over a 50-year period, and in 2006 he released *Book of Longing* alongside a new album, *Blue Alert*. Dylan, however, has attracted the most sustained attention from critics. He has been linked with the troubadour tradition, the metaphysical poets, Blake, Allan Ginsberg and William Burroughs, and it is clear that his songs can be read in a literary context. He is well aware of the conventions of the lyric mode that are closely associated with music (the love song or the religious poem), and his work makes extensive use of literary allusion. Equally, as Christopher Ricks, Neil Corcoran and others have shown, his lyrics can be studied as written poetry (Corcoran 2002; Ricks 2003). Aidan Day argues, for example, that Dylan's lyrics construct an author–reader relationship that hinges on the incitement and simultaneous frustration of readerly desire (Day 1988), making them reminiscent of the courtly love poem. Dylan's songs play with, and often reverse, the conventions of courtly lyric, from the sly seduction of 'I'll Be Your Baby Tonight' to 'It Ain't Me Babe', which rejects 'the bourgeois idea of the settled relationship' and 'scrutinizes, with devastating honesty, the inability of the singer to measure up to the ideal proposed by the woman' (Corcoran 2002: 19–20). Dylan's exploitation of these courtly conventions perhaps discloses a deeper historical affinity with the early modern. As Elizabeth Heale suggests, the courtly lyric resembles contemporary popular music: despite its sometimes lofty register, it is concerned with love and erotic desire, social comment, and 'self-promotion and public image making' (Heale 1998: 3).

Yet, in many respects, Dylan's songs resist the confines of the printed page. Corcoran remarks that his printed lyrics often bear little relation to what he sings, either on officially released versions or in any individual performance (Corcoran 2002: 15). The original 'text' of a Dylan song is also hard to establish, as in each song words and music interact with the performing voice and the performance context. Dylan often breaks lines at different points from the written lyrics, for expressive effect, and there is great variation in his catalogue of songs, leaving them open to revision and reinterpretation by the performer and the audience/critic. Dylan's particular contribution to the history of lyric resides in the integral connection with popular culture, periodic links with political dissent, and his style of performance, which foregrounds spontaneity, variation and disrupted temporality.

The diverse racial and ethnic composition of post-war Britain has intensified the interaction of lyric and music. Black British poets such as Linton Kwesi Johnson, Grace Nicholls, Fred D'Aguiar and Benjamin Zephaniah have transformed the linguistic texture of lyric poetry. Johnson's 'dub' style fuses reggae rhythms and oral poetry: as he points out, '[t]he music's there in the structure of the speech. I always have a bass line at the back of my mind when I write' (quoted by Childs 1999: 199). Johnson toured with a band and sound system in the 1970s, and Zephaniah has taken on this performance style as a mode of cultural resistance. (The challenge to Standard English and traditional poetic idiom mounted by these poets is echoed in the Scottish vernacular speech deployed by Tom Leonard and Liz Lochead.) The polemical quality of such poetry poses some problems for conventional literary criticism. Philip Hobsbaum argues that in the performance poetry of Zephaniah and others, '[t]he meaning is being pushed into the text by the performer, not being drawn out of it by the reader' (Hobsbaum 1996: 183). The act of interpretation supplants the text, which is 'recreated each time a new performer chooses to realise it'. Hobsbaum distinguishes this situation from that of literary texts, where we have 'the sensation of hearing the voices of their authors' (*ibid*.: 184): the intention behind the written poem is thus preserved. This study has shown the difficulty of sustaining this distinction: the lyric 'I' is a fictive presence, and both oral and written poems involve an act of performance by the speaking voice and by the addressee/reader/listener.

Mainstream poetic practice has also been effective in harnessing the contemporary appetite for performed poetry, a fact illustrated by the launch in November 2005 of the Poetry Archive (www. poetryarchive.org), an online resource containing recordings of poets reading their work. The Poet Laureate Andrew Motion, one of the Archive's Directors, observed that 'the present resurgence of public poetry readings is not so much a new phenomenon, but a return to a very ancient tradition – one which runs all the way back to the Beowulf poet in his mead hall, and beyond' (Motion 2005: 13). Motion invokes epic and heroic traditions here, but the connection between voice and word, performance and poetry is equally strong in the history of lyric, and most of the poets recorded in the Archive write in a recognisably lyric mode.

The term 'popular' is historically variable, and one must guard against the 'myth-making nostalgia' (Lindley 1985: 22) that anchors lyric in communal practices. Yet this book has demonstrated that lyric consistently retains a link to popular entertainments and rituals through its relation to music and performance. Lyric is not just a facet of 'high' culture; it filters into 'everyday life' in ways that more elaborate literary and musical forms do not. As Theodor Adorno contends:

> A collective undercurrent provides the foundation for all individual lyric poetry. When that poetry actually bears the whole in mind and is not simply an expression of the privilege, refinement, and gentility of those who can afford to be gentle, participation in this undercurrent is an essential part of the substantiality of the individual lyric as well.
>
> (Adorno 1974: 45).

The lyric, one might say, is most itself when it goes beyond the self.

Glossary

Anaphora   A rhetorical device used in poetry and prose, in which a word or phrase is repeated in a number of successive clauses. It is often associated with attempts to persuade, or with the expression of powerful emotion. Shylock's speech in Act III of *The Merchant of Venice* exemplifies the rhetorical power of repetition: 'If you prick us, do we not bleed? if you tickle us, do we not laugh? if you poison us, do we not die? and if you wrong us, shall we not revenge? If we are like you in the rest, we will resemble you in that.'

Ballad   A song or poem that tells a story, often in colloquial language, and that is associated with popular and folk culture. Originally meaning a dancing song, the ballad lends itself to performance, with the narrative and tune subject to alteration. The traditional oral ballad is typically characterised by dramatic action, dialogue and third-person narration. The broadside ballad appeared in print form and dealt with topical events. In the eighteenth century, the literary ballad became increasingly common: it imitated the traditional ballad form and was a major influence on Romantic lyric.

Bard   In Celtic cultures, an official poet whose role was to celebrate and commemorate heroic actions. The figure of the bard embodies the ancient associations of poetry with song and prophetic power.

Blazon   A poetic device that describes a woman's beauty by listing her physical features.

Caesura   A pause within a line of verse. In English verse, the pause may fall between a metrical foot, or it may divide feet. The pause can fall around the middle of a line (medial), but it can also be placed towards the beginning (initial) or near the end (terminal). There may be one or more of these breaks in a single line of verse. The following line from Sir Thomas Wyatt's 'They Flee From Me' has a medial caesura: 'It was no dream, I lay broad waking.' In contrast, Shakespeare's Sonnet 129 deploys heavy internal pauses: 'lust/ Is perjured, murd'rous, bloody, full of blame,/ Savage, extreme, rude, cruel, not to trust.'

Carol   Originally a round dance accompanied by music and song, and in the medieval period a love song or religious poem. Now denotes a joyous Christmas hymn.

Carpe diem   A Latin phrase, meaning 'seize the day', from one of the Roman poet Horace's *Odes*. The *carpe diem* motif involves a plea to enjoy youthful pleasures, since life is short and time is fleeting. Two notable examples are Andrew Marvell's 'To His Coy Mistress' and Robert Herrick's 'To the Virgins, to Make Much of Time', which contains the famous line 'Gather ye Rose-buds while ye may'.

Conceit   A figurative device that proposes an unexpected parallel between apparently dissimilar things, ideas or situations. The Petrarchan conceit, a common feature in Elizabethan poetry, makes exaggerated claims for the poet's beloved. Metaphysical poets such as John Donne are particularly noted for their witty and extravagant conceits.

Didactic literature   Literature that is designed to teach or provide guidance, either by conveying practical knowledge or by providing moral and religious instruction. The majority of medieval poetry had a didactic purpose.

Epic   A long narrative poem that adopts an elevated style, and that involves divine, mythological or superhuman heroes and events. Traditional or primary epics such as Homer's *Iliad* (eighth century BCE) or the Anglo-Saxon *Beowulf* (eighth century) are closely tied to the oral traditions of a tribe or people, while literary epics such as the Roman poet Virgil's *Aeneid* (30–20 BCE), the medieval Italian Dante's *Divine Comedy* (1307–21), Edmund Spenser's *The Faerie Queene* (1589–96) or John Milton's *Paradise Lost* (1667) imitate these earlier models, but are written by a single author for a literate readership.

Epideictic   Rhetorical language used for public praise and display.

Epigram   A short, witty and polished statement in verse or prose, often deployed for commemorative, celebratory, humorous or satirical effect. Alexander Pope's 'Epitaph. Intended for Sir Isaac Newton, In Westminster Abbey' combines several of these functions: 'Nature, and Nature's Laws lay hid in Night./ God said, *Let Newton be!* and All was *Light*.'

Homily   A short sermon or discourse on a religious or moral topic. Much medieval verse was homiletic in character.

Iambic   The most common metrical foot in English verse. It consists of a light or weak stress followed by a strong stress, and is sometimes called a rising rhythm. The opening line of Christina Rossetti's 'An Apple-Gathering' uses the iambic foot: 'I plucked pink blossoms from mine apple tree.'

Neoplatonism   A school of Platonic philosophy, based on Plato's theories of love, which originated in the third century. It promoted the idea that beauty, goodness and truth in the world emanate from the One or Absolute, the eternal, transcendent source of all value. Neoplatonism heavily influenced Renaissance Christian thought, which blended the concept of the Absolute with that of God. In the love poetry of the medieval and early modern periods, the Platonic lover is attracted to the physical beauty of the Beloved, but this outer appearance is merely a manifestation of a higher, spiritual beauty. Thus the lover's erotic desire is transformed into the contemplation and veneration of the Divine.

Ode   A form of lyric poetry typified by its serious purpose, elevated style and elaborate stanzaic forms. The main types of ode in English poetry are the Pindaric or regular, the irregular, and the Horatian. The Pindaric ode, following the model of the Greek poet Pindar, praises or eulogises a person, art form or concept, and maintains a consistent set of stanzaic patterns. The irregular ode, developed by Abraham Cowley in the mid-seventeenth century, varies the line lengths, number of lines and rhyme schemes of each stanza, a structure that enables shifts in mood and subject matter. The Horatian ode, following the example of the Roman poet Horace, tends to be more meditative and subjective.

Orientalism   A term coined by the post-colonial critic Edward Said, who defines it as 'a Western style for dominating, restructuring, and having authority over the Orient'. Orientalism involves the ideological construction of 'the Orient' through artistic, political, economic, historical and philological discourses and practices.

Panegyric   A public speech or poem of praise; from the Greek, meaning 'public assembly'.

Pentameter   In verse, a line consisting of five metrical feet. The iambic pentameter, whether rhymed or unrhymed, is the most common metre in English poetry. The opening lines from Shakespeare's Sonnet 71 are an example of iambic pentameter: 'No longer mourn for me when I am dead/ Than you shall hear the surly sullen bell'.

Rhetoric The art of speaking and writing in order to persuade an audience. Aristotle, Cicero and Quintilian were prominent theorists of rhetoric in classical antiquity. Elaborate rules and techniques were devised for composing and delivering speeches, and the figurative language deployed by orators was also subject to extensive classification and analysis.

Rondeau An intricate French verse form, usually consisting of 13 lines and deploying only two rhymes. The opening words are used as a refrain, and recur after the eighth and 13th lines.

Soliloquy A dramatic device in which a character directly addresses the audience, revealing his or her motivations and feelings: it is as if the character is thinking aloud. The soliloquies in Christopher Marlowe's *Dr Faustus*, and Shakespeare's *Macbeth* and *Hamlet*, are among the best known examples.

Sonnet A lyric poem consisting of 14 lines of rhymed iambic pentameter. The sonnet can be divided into an octave (eight lines) and a sestet (six lines), or alternatively three quatrains (four lines) and a closing couplet. The sonnet originated in Italy and came to England via France in the sixteenth century. It has served a variety of amatory, religious and philosophical purposes. The three main sonnet patterns are the Petrarchan, with an octave and sestet, rhymed *abbaabba cdecde* (or *cdcdcd*); the Spenserian, with three quatrains and a couplet, rhymed *abab, bcbc, cdcd, ee*; and the Shakespearean, again with three quatrains and a couplet, but rhymed *abab, cdcd, efef, gg*. George Meredith's *Modern Love* (1862) deployed a 16-line sonnet, a form taken up by Tony Harrison in the contemporary period.

Tetrameter In verse, a line consisting of four metrical feet, and one of the most common metres in English poetry. The following lines from William Wordsworth's 'The Solitary Reaper' are in iambic tetrameter: 'Alone she cuts and binds the grain,/ And sings a melancholy strain'.

Trochaic A metrical foot consisting of a strong stress followed by a light or weak stress, and is also known as falling rhythm, in contrast to the rising rhythm of the iambic stress. Trochaic lines often leave out the last unstressed syllable, as in William Blake's 'The Tyger': 'Tyger! Tyger! Burning bright'. Such lines are termed 'catalectic'.

Bibliography

Primary sources

Alexander, Michael (trans.) (1973) *Beowulf*, Harmondsworth: Penguin.

Arnold, Matthew (1979) *Poems*, 2nd edn, ed. Miriam Allott, London: Longman.

Ault, Norman (ed.) (1949) *Elizabethan Lyrics*, London: Longmans, Green and Co.

Barrett Browning, Elizabeth (1995) *Aurora Leigh and Other Poems*, eds John Robert Glorney Bolton and Julia Bolton Holloway, Harmondsworth: Penguin.

Behn, Aphra (1992) *Works Vol. 1: Poetry*, ed. Janet Todd, London: Pickering.

Bradley, S. A. J. (trans. and ed.) (1982) *Anglo-Saxon Poetry*, London: Everyman.

Brooks, Chris and Peter Faulkner (eds) (1996) *The White Man's Burden: British Poetry of the Empire*, Exeter: University of Exeter Press.

Brown, Andy (ed.) (2006) *The Allotment: New Lyric Poets*, Exeter: Stride.

Browning, Robert (1988) *The Poetical Works, Vol. 3*, eds Ian Jack and Rowena Fowler, Oxford: Clarendon Press.

Caddel, Richard and Peter Quartermain (eds) (1999) *Other: British and Irish Poetry since 1970*, Middletown, CT, USA: Wesleyan University Press.

Clare, John (1967) *Selected Poems and Prose*, eds Eric Robinson and Geoffrey Summerfield, London: Oxford University Press.

Cowley, Abraham (1905) *Poems*, ed. A. R. Waller, Cambridge: Cambridge University Press.

Crossley-Holland, Kevin (ed.) (1984) *The Anglo-Saxon World: An Anthology*, Oxford: Oxford University Press.

Day Lewis, C. (ed.) (1961) *English Lyric Poems 1500–1900*, New York: Appleton.

Davie, Donald (ed.) (1974) *Augustan Lyric*, London, Heinemann.

Davies, R. T. (ed.) (1963) *Medieval English Lyrics: A Critical Anthology*, London: Faber.

Donne, John (1985) *The Complete English Poems*, ed. C. A. Patrides, London: J. M. Dent.

Duffy, Carol Ann (2005) *Rapture*, London: Picador.

—— (2006) *Selected Poems*, Harmondsworth: Penguin.

Dylan, Bob (2004) *Lyrics 1962–2001*, New York and London: Simon and Schuster.

Eliot, T. S. (1985) *Collected Poems 1909–1962*, London: Faber.

Fullard, Joyce (ed.) (1990) *British Women Poets 1660–1800: An Anthology*, New York: Whitson.

Gurney, Ivor (2004) *Collected Poems*, ed. P. J. Kavanagh, Manchester: Carcanet.

Hardy, Thomas (1923) *Collected Poems*, 2nd edn, London: Macmillan.

Heaney, Seamus (1966) *Death of a Naturalist*, London: Faber.

Hill, Geoffrey (1986) *Collected Poems*, Oxford: Oxford University Press.

Jones, Peter (ed.) (1972) *Imagist Poetry*, Harmondsworth: Penguin.

Keats, John (1977) *The Complete Poems*, 2nd edn, ed. John Barnard, Harmondsworth: Penguin.

Larkin, Philip (1988) *Collected Poems*, ed. Anthony Thwaite, London: Faber.

Marvell, Andrew (2003) *Poems*, ed. Nigel Smith, Edinburgh: Pearson.

Moore, Geoffrey (ed.) (1983) *The Penguin Book of American Verse*, rev. edn., Harmondsworth: Penguin.

Olson, Elder (ed.) (1964) *American Lyric Poems: From Colonial Times to the Present*, New York: Appleton.

Palgrave, Francis Turner (ed.) (1964) *The Golden Treasury* [1861], 5th edn, ed. John Press, Oxford: Oxford University Press.

Philips, Katherine (1990) *The Collected Works, Vol. 1: The Poems*, ed. Patrick Thomas, Stump Cross: Stump Cross Books.

Plath, Sylvia (1981) *Collected Poems*, London: Faber.

Pope, Alexander (1954) *Poems, Vol. VI: Minor Poems*, eds Norman Ault and John Butt, London: Methuen.

—— (1993) *Major Works*, ed. Pat Rogers, Oxford: Oxford University Press.

Press, Alan R. (ed. and trans.) (1971) *Anthology of Troubadour Lyric Poetry*, Edinburgh: Edinburgh University Press.

Rees-Jones, Deryn (ed.) (2005) *Modern Women Poets*, Newcastle: Bloodaxe.

Reeves, James (ed.) (1981) *Georgian Poetry*, Harmondsworth: Penguin.

Ricks, Christopher (ed.) (1999) *The Oxford Book of English Verse*, Oxford: Oxford University Press.

Riley, Denise (1993) *Mop Mop Georgette: New and Selected Poems 1986–1993*, Cambridge: Reality Street.

Rosenberg, Isaac (1979) *The Collected Works: Poetry, Prose, Letters, Paintings and Drawings*, ed. Ian Parsons, London: Chatto and Windus.

Sexton, Anne (1971) *Transformations*, Boston: Houghton Mifflin.

Shakespeare, William (1997) *Macbeth*, ed. A. R. Braunmuller, Cambridge: Cambridge University Press.

—— (2006) *The Sonnets*, ed. G. Blakemore Evans, Cambridge: Cambridge University Press.

Shelley, Percy Bysshe (2002) *Poetry and Prose*, 2nd edn, eds Donald H. Reiman and Neil Fraistat, New York: Norton.

Sidney, Philip (1962) *Poems*, ed. William A. Ringler Jr, Oxford: Clarendon Press.

Tennyson, Alfred (1989) *A Selected Edition*, ed. Christopher Ricks, London: Longman.

Thomas, Edward (1985) *Collected Poems*, London: Faber.

Thomas, R. S. (1994) *Selected Poems 1948–1968*, Newcastle, Bloodaxe.

Wordsworth, Dorothy (1991) *The Grasmere Journals*, ed. Pamela Woof, Oxford: Clarendon Press.

Wordsworth, William (1986) *Major Works*, ed. Stephen Gill, Oxford: Oxford University Press.

—— (1992) *Lyrical Ballads*, ed. Michael Mason, London: Longman.

Yeats, W. B. (1982) *Collected Poems*, Basingstoke: Macmillan.

Secondary sources

Abrams, M. H. (1953) *The Mirror and the Lamp: Romantic Theory and the Critical Tradition*, New York: Oxford University Press.

—— (1970) 'Structure and Style in the Greater Romantic Lyric', in F. W. Hilles and Harold Bloom (eds) *From Sensibility to Romanticism*, Oxford: Oxford University Press, 527–60.

—— (1993) *A Glossary of Literary Terms*, 6th edn, Fort Worth, TX, USA: Harcourt Brace.

Adorno, Theodor W. (1974) 'On Lyric Poetry and Society' [1957], in Rolf Tiedemann (ed.), Sherry Weber Nicholsen (trans.), *Notes to Literature Vol. 1*, New York: Columbia University Press, 37–54.

Aristotle (1996) *Poetics*, trans. Malcolm Heath, Harmondsworth: Penguin.

Austin, J. L. (1962) *How to do Things with Words*, Oxford: Clarendon Press.

Barthes, Roland (1993) *A Roland Barthes Reader*, ed. Susan Sontag, London: Vintage.

Belsey, Catherine (1999) 'John Donne's Worlds of Desire', in Mousley, A. (ed.) *John Donne: New Casebooks*, Basingstoke: Macmillan, 63–80.

Benjamin, Walter (1983) *Charles Baudelaire: A Lyric Poet in the Era of High Capitalism*, trans. Harry Zohn, London: Verso.

Bergstrom, Carson (2002) *The Rise of New Science: Epistemological, Linguistic, and Ethical Ideals and the Lyric of Genre in the Eighteenth Century*, Lampeter and Lewiston, New York: Edwin Mellen.

Blevins, Jacob (2004) *Catullan Consciousness and the Early Modern Lyric in England: From Wyatt to Donne*, Aldershot: Ashgate.

Bloom, Harold (1979) 'The Breaking of Form', in Harold Bloom *et al.* (eds) *Deconstruction and Criticism*, New York: Continuum, 1–38.

Bold, Alan (1979) *The Ballad*, London: Methuen.

Bradford, Richard (1993) *A Linguistic History of English Poetry*, London: Routledge.

Bristow, Joseph (ed.) (1987) *The Victorian Poet: Poetics and Persona*, London: Croom Helm.

Brooks, Cleanth (1968) *The Well-Wrought Urn*, London: Methuen.

Brooks, Cleanth and Robert Penn Warren (1976) *Understanding Poetry*, 4th edn, New York: Holt, Rinehart and Winston.

Brooks, Jean (1971) *Thomas Hardy: The Poetic Structure*, Ithaca: Cornell University Press.

Brooks, Peter (1984) *Reading for the Plot: Design and Invention in Narrative*, Cambridge, MA, USA: Harvard University Press.

Broom, Sarah (2006) *Contemporary British and Irish Poetry*, London: Palgrave.

Byron, Glennis (2003) *Dramatic Monologue*, London: Routledge.

Cameron, Sharon (1979) *Lyric Time: Dickinson and the Limits of Genre*, Baltimore and London: Johns Hopkins University Press.

Chase, Cynthia (1985) '"Viewless Wings": Intertextual Interpretation of Keats's "Ode to a Nightingale"', in Chaviva Hosek and Patricia Parker (eds) *Lyric Poetry: Beyond New Criticism*, Ithaca and London: Cornell University Press, 208–25.

Childs, Peter (1999) *The Twentieth Century in Poetry: A Critical Survey*, London: Routledge.

Cohen, J. M. (1963) *The Baroque Lyric*, London: Hutchinson.

Coleridge, Samuel Taylor (2004) *Poetry and Prose: Authoritative Texts, Criticism*. ed. Nicholas Halmi, Paul Magnuson and Raimonda Modiano, New York: Norton.

Collecott, Diana (1985) 'Remembering Oneself: The Reputation and Later Poetry of H.D', *Critical Quarterly* 27 (1): 7–22.

Cook, Jon (ed.) (2004) *Poetry in Theory: An Anthology 1900–2000*, Oxford: Blackwell.

Corcoran, Neil (ed.) (2002) *Do You, Mr Jones? Bob Dylan with the Poets and Professors*, London: Chatto and Windus.

Corns, Thomas N. (ed.) (1998) *The Cambridge Companion to English Poetry, Donne to Marvell*, Cambridge: Cambridge University Press.

—— (1998) 'The Poetry of the Caroline Court', *Proceedings of the British Academy* 97: 51–73.

Cox, Philip (1996) *Gender, Genre and the Romantic Poets: An Introduction*, Manchester: Manchester University Press.

Creaser, John (1998) 'John Keats, Odes', in Duncan Wu (ed.) *A Companion to Romanticism*, Oxford: Blackwell, 237–46.

Culler, Jonathan (1975) *Structuralist Poetics: Structuralism, Linguistics and the Study of Literature*, London: Routledge and Kegan Paul.

—— (1981) *The Pursuit of Signs: Semiotics, Literature, Deconstruction*, London: Routledge.

—— (1985) 'Changes in the Study of Lyric', in Hosek and Parker (eds), *op. cit.*, 38–54.

Curran, Stuart (1986) *Poetic Form and British Romanticism*, Oxford: Oxford University Press.

Day, Aidan (1988) *Jokerman: Reading the Lyrics of Bob Dylan*, Oxford: Blackwell.

Day Lewis, C. (1965) *The Lyric Impulse*, London: Chatto and Windus.

Dickie, Margaret (1991) *Lyric Contingencies: Emily Dickinson and Wallace Stevens*, Philadelphia: University of Pennsylvania Press.

Dronke, Peter (1968) *The Medieval Lyric*, London: Hutchinson.

Duff, Davie (ed.) (2000) *Modern Genre Theory*, London: Longman.

DuPlessis, Rachel Blau (1990) *The Pink Guitar: Writing as Feminist Practice*, London: Routledge.

Easthope, Antony (1983) *Poetry and Discourse*, London: Methuen.

—— (1989) *Poetry and Phantasy*, Cambridge: Cambridge University Press.

Eliot, T. S. (1990) *On Poetry and Poets* [1957], London: Faber.

Ellmann, Maud (1987) *The Poetics of Impersonality: T.S. Eliot and Ezra Pound*, Hemel Hempstead: Harvester.

Finnegan, Ruth (1977) *Oral Poetry: Its Nature, Significance and Social Context*, Cambridge: Cambridge University Press.

Fontanier, Pierre (1968) *Les Figures du Discours* [1830], Paris: Flammarion.

Fowler, Alistair (1982) *Kinds of Literature: An Introduction to the Theory of Genres and Modes*, Oxford: Clarendon.

Frow, John (2006) *Genre*, London, Routledge.

Frye, Northrop (1957) *Anatomy of Criticism*, Princeton, NJ, USA: Princeton University Press.

Furniss, Tom and Michael Bath (1996) *Reading Poetry: An Introduction*, Hemel Hempstead: Harvester.

Gardner, Helen (1949) *The Art of T. S. Eliot*, London: Cresset Press.

Genette, Gérard (1992) *The Architext: An Introduction*, trans. Jane E. Lewin, Berkeley: University of California Press.

Gittings, Robert (ed.) (1985) *Letters of John Keats*, Oxford: Oxford University Press.

Grady, Hugh H. (1981) 'Notes on Marxism and the Lyric', *Contemporary Literature* 22 (4): 544–55.

Gray, Douglas (1972) *Themes and Images in the Medieval English Lyric*, London: Routledge and Kegan Paul.

Greenblatt, Stephen (1980) *Renaissance Self-Fashioning: From More to Shakespeare*, Chicago and London: University of Chicago Press.

Gregory, Eileen (2003) 'H. D.'s Heterodoxy: the Lyric as a Site of Resistance', in Marina Camboni (ed.) *H. D.'s Poetry: 'The Meanings that Words Hide'*, New York: AMS Press, 21–33.

Halpern, Richard (1999) 'The Lyric in the Field of Information: Autopoesis and History in Donne's *Songs and Sonnets*', in Mousley (ed.), *op. cit.*, 104–21.

Hardy, Barbara (1977) *The Advantage of Lyric: Essays on Feeling in Poetry*, London: Athlone.

Harrison, Tony (1987) *Selected Poems*, Harmondsworth: Penguin.

Harvey, A. E. (1955) 'The Classification of Greek Lyric Poetry', *The Classical Quarterly* 5 (3): 157–75.

Heale, Elizabeth (1998) *Wyatt, Surrey and Early Tudor Poetry*, London: Longman.

Hernandi, Paul (1972) *Beyond Genre*, Ithaca: Cornell University Press.

Hobsbaum, Philip (1996) *Metre, Rhythm and Verse Form*, London: Routledge.

Holden, Jonathan (1981) *The Rhetoric of Contemporary Lyric*, Bloomington, IN, USA: Indiana University Press.

Holloway, John (1968) *Blake: The Lyric Poetry*, London: Edward Arnold.

Hosek, Chaviva and Patricia Parker (eds) (1985) *Lyric Poetry: Beyond New Criticism*, Ithaca and London: Cornell University Press.

Hough, Graham (1960) *Image and Experience*, London: Duckworth.

Howe, Elisabeth A. (1996) *The Dramatic Monologue*, New York: Twayne.

Hunt, Clay (1954) *Donne's Poetry: Essays in Literary Analysis*, New Haven, CT, USA: Yale University Press.

Ing, Catherine (1951) *Elizabethan Lyrics*, London: Chatto and Windus.

Janowitz, Anne (1998) *Lyric and Labour in the Romantic Tradition*, Cambridge: Cambridge University Press.

Jauss, Hans Robert (1982) *Toward an Aesthetic of Reception*, trans. Timothy Bahti, Minneapolis: University of Minnesota Press.

Jeffreys, Mark (1995) 'Ideologies of Lyric: A Problem of Genre in Contemporary Anglophone Poetics', *PMLA* 110 (2): 196–205.

Johnson, Barbara (1991) 'Apostrophe, Animation, and Abortion', in Robyn R. Warhol and Diane Price Herndl (eds), *Feminisms: An Anthology of Literary Theory and Criticism*, New Brunswick, NJ, USA: Rutgers University Press, 630–43.

Johnson, W. R. (1982) *The Idea of Lyric: Lyric Modes in Ancient and Modern Poetry*, Berkeley: University of California Press.

Johnston, John H. (1964) *English Poetry of the First World War: A Study in the Evolution of Lyric and Narrative Form*, Princeton, NJ, USA: Princeton University Press/Oxford University Press.

Kinnahan, Linda A. (1996) 'Experimental Poetics and the Lyric in British Women's Poetry: Geraldine Monk, Wendy Mulford and Denise Riley', *Contemporary Literature* 37 (4): 620–70.

Kolocotroni, Vassiliki, Jane Goldman and Olga Taxidou (eds) (1998) *Modernism: An Anthology of Sources and Documents*, Edinburgh: Edinburgh University Press.

Kidd, Helen (1993) 'The Paper City: Women, Writing and Experience', in Robert Hampson and Peter Barry (eds), *New British Poetries: The Scope of the Possible*, Manchester: Manchester University Press, 156–80.

Langbaum, Robert (1957) *The Poetry of Experience: The Dramatic Monologue in Modern Literary Tradition*, Chicago: Chicago University Press.

Latane, David E. Jr. (1999) 'Literary Criticism', in Tucker (ed.) *op. cit.*, 388–405.

Lewalski, Barbara Keifer (1979) *Protestant Poetics and the Seventeenth-Century Religious Lyric*, Princeton, NJ, USA: Princeton University Press.

Lever, Julius Walter (1956) *The Elizabethan Love Sonnet*, 2nd edn, London: Methuen.

Lindley, David (1985) *Lyric*, London and New York: Methuen.

—— (1990) 'Lyric', in Martin Coyle, Peter Garside, Malcolm Kelsall and John Peck (eds), *Encyclopedia of Literature and Criticism*, London: Routledge, 188–98.

Longley, Edna (2005) 'The Great War, History and the English Lyric', in Vincent Sherry (ed.) *The Cambridge Companion to the Literature of the First World War*, Cambridge: Cambridge University Press, 57–84.

Lord, Albert B. (1960) *The Singer of Tales*, Cambridge, MA, USA.: Harvard University Press.

Low, Donald A. (ed.) (1974) *Robert Burns: The Critical Heritage*, London: Routledge.

Lukács, Georg (1978) *The Theory of the Novel*, London: Merlin Press.

MacLean, Norman (1952) 'From Action to Image: Theories of the Lyric in the Eighteenth Century', in R. S. Crane (ed.), *Critics and Criticism*, Chicago: Chicago University Press, 408–60.

de Man, Paul (1983) *Blindness and Insight: Essays in the Rhetoric of Contemporary Criticism*, 2nd rev. edn, Minneapolis, MN, USA: University of Minnesota Press.

—— (1984) *The Rhetoric of Romanticism*, New York: Columbia University Press.

—— (1985) 'Lyrical Voice in Contemporary Theory: Riffaterre and Jauss', in Hosek and Parker (eds), *op. cit.*, 55–72.

Marinetti, Filippo Tommaso (1972) *Selected Writings*, ed. and trans. R. W. Flint, New York: Farrar, Strauss and Giroux.

Mark, Alison and Deryn Rees-Jones (eds) (2000) *Contemporary Women's Poetry: Reading/Writing/Practice*, London: Palgrave.

Marotti, Arthur (1991) 'The Transmission of Lyric Poetry and the Institutionalizing of Literature in the English Renaissance', in Marie-Rose Logan and Peter L. Rudnytsky (eds), *Contending Kingdoms: Historical, Psychological, and Feminist Approaches to the Literature of Sixteenth-Century England and France*, Detroit: Wayne State University Press, 27–47.

Matterson, Stephen and Darryl Jones (2000) *Studying Poetry*, London: Arnold.

McGann, Jerome (1998) 'Byron and the Anonymous Lyric', in Wu (ed.), *op. cit.*, 243–60.

Middleton, Peter (1993) 'Who am I to Speak?: The Politics of Subjectivity in Recent British Poetry', in Robert Hampson and Peter Barry (eds), *New British Poetries: The Scope of the Possible*, Manchester: Manchester University Press, 107–33.

Middleton, Peter and Tim Woods (2000) *Literatures of Memory: History, Time and Space in Post-War Writing*, Manchester: Manchester University Press.

Mill, John Stuart (1973) 'What is Poetry?' [1833, 1859], in Lionel Trilling and Harold Bloom (eds) *The Oxford Anthology of English Literature: Victorian Prose and Poetry*, Oxford: Oxford University Press, 76–83.

—— (1989) 'The Two Kinds of Poetry' [1833], in Peter Faulkner (ed.), *A Victorian Reader*, London: Batsford, 50–64.

Motion, Andrew (2005) 'All in the Ear', *Times Literary Supplement*, November 25: 13.

Mousley, Andrew (ed.) (1999) *John Donne: New Casebooks*, Basingstoke: Macmillan.

Munns, Jessica (2004) 'Pastoral and Lyric: Astrea in Arcadia', in Derek Hughes and Janet Todd (eds), *The Cambridge Companion to Aphra Behn*, Cambridge: Cambridge University Press, 204–20.

Mulford, Wendy. (1983) 'Notes on Writing: A Marxist/Feminist Viewpoint', in Michele Wandor (ed.), *On Gender and Writing*, London: Pandora, 31–41.

Patey, Douglas Lane (1993) '"Aesthetics" and the Rise of Lyric in the Eighteenth Century', *Studies in English Literature 1500–1900* 33 (3): 587–608.

Parfitt, George (1992) *English Poetry of the Seventeenth Century*, 2nd edn, London: Longman.

Perloff, Marjorie (1985) *The Dance of the Intellect: Studies in the Poetry of the Pound Tradition*, New York: Cambridge University Press.

—— (1990) *Poetic Licence: Essays on Modernist and Postmodernist Lyric*, Evanston, IL: Northwestern University Press.

Perry, Seamus (2002) 'The Talker', in Lucy Newlyn (ed.), *The Cambridge Companion to Coleridge*, Cambridge: Cambridge University Press, 103–25.

Peterson, Douglas L. (1967) *The English Lyric from Wyatt to Donne: A History of the Plain and Eloquent Styles*, Princeton, NJ, USA: Princeton University Press.

Plato (1987) *The Republic*, trans. Desmond Lee, Harmondsworth: Penguin.

Poe, Edgar Allan (1984) *Essays and Reviews*, New York: Viking.

Pound, Ezra (1961) *ABC of Reading*, London: Faber.

—— (1970) *Gaudier-Breska*, New York: New Directions.

Preminger, Alex and T. V. F. Brogan (eds) (1993) *Princeton Encyclopaedia of Poetry and Poetics*, Princeton, NJ, USA: Princeton University Press.

Prins, Yopie (1999) *Victorian Sappho*, Princeton, NJ, USA: Princeton University Press.

Rader, Ralph (1976) 'The Dramatic Monologue and Related Lyric Forms', *Critical Inquiry* 3 (1): 131–51.

—— (1984) 'Notes on Some Structural Varieties and Variations in Dramatic "I" Poems and Their Theoretical Implications', *Victorian Poetry* 22 (2): 103–20.

Rajan, Tillotama (1985) 'Romanticism and the Death of Lyric Consciousness', in Hosek and Parker (eds), *op. cit.*, 194–207.

Ramazani, Jahan (1994) *Poetry of Mourning: The Modern Elegy from Hardy to Heaney*, Chicago and London: University of Chicago Press.

Rees-Jones, Deryn (2005) *Consorting with Angels: Essays on Modern Women Poets*, Newcastle, Bloodaxe.

Rhys, Ernest (1913) *Lyric Poetry*, London, J. M. Dent.

Ricks, Christopher (2003) *Dylan's Visions of Sin*, London: Viking.

Riley, Denise (2000) *The Words of Selves*, Stanford, CA, USA: Stanford University Press.

Roberts, Neil (1999) *Narrative and Voice in Postwar Poetry*, London: Longman.

Rose, Jacqueline (2003) *On Not Being Able to Sleep: Psychoanalysis and the Modern World*, London: Chatto and Windus.

Ross, Andrew (1991) 'Poetry and Motion: Madonna and Public Enemy', in Antony Easthope and John. O. Thompson (eds), *Contemporary Poetry Meets Modern Theory*, Hemel Hempstead: Harvester, 96–107.

Ruoff, Gene W. (1989) *Wordsworth and Coleridge: The Making of the Major Lyrics 1802–1804*, London: Harvester.

Sacks, Peter M. (1985) *The English Elegy: Readings in the Genre from Spenser to Yeats*, Baltimore, MD, USA: Johns Hopkins University Press.

Schelling, Frederic E. (1913) *The English Lyric*, London: Constable.

Shuster, George N. (1940) *The English Ode from Milton to Keats*, New York: Columbia University Press.

Scodel, Joshua (1998) 'Lyric Forms', in Steven N. Zwicker (ed.), *The Cambridge Companion to English Literature 1650–1740*, Cambridge: Cambridge University Press: 118–42.

Scully, James (ed.) (1966) *Modern Poets on Modern Poetry*, London: Fontana.

Sedgwick, W. B. (1924) 'The Lyric Impulse', *Music & Letters* 5 (2): 97–102.

Sessions, Ina Beth (1947) 'The Dramatic Monologue', *PMLA* 62: 503–16.

Shaw, W. David. (1997) 'Lyric Displacement in the Victorian Monologue: Naturalizing the Vocative', *Nineteenth-Century Literature* 52 (3): 302–25.

Sidney, Philip (1965) *An Apology for Poetry* [1595], ed. Geoffrey Shepherd, London: Nelson.

Sinclair, May (1915) 'Two Notes', *Egoist* 11 (1 June).

Sinfield, Alan (1977) *Dramatic Monologue*, London: Methuen.

Slinn, E. Warwick (1999) 'Poetry', in H. F. Tucker (ed.) *A Companion to Victorian Literature and Culture*, Oxford: Blackwell, 307–22.

Smith, Barbara Hernstein (1978) *On the Margins of Discourse*, Chicago: Chicago University Press.

Spiller, Michael (1992) *The Development of the Sonnet*, London and New York: Routledge.

Stein, Arnold (1962) *John Donne's Lyrics: The Eloquence of Action*, Minneapolis: University of Minnesota Press.

Stevens, John (1979) *Music and Poetry in the Early Tudor Court*, London: Methuen.

Targoff, Ramie (2001) *Common Prayer: The Language of Public Devotion in Early Modern England*, Chicago and London: University of Chicago Press.

Tarlo, Harriet (2000) '"A She Even Smaller Than a Me": Gender Dramas of the Contemporary Avant-Garde', in Mark and Rees-Jones (eds), *op. cit.*, 247–70.

Thacker, Andrew (1993) 'Imagist Travels in Modernist Space', *Textual Practice* 7 (2): 224–46.

Tiffany, Daniel (2001) 'Lyric Substance: On Riddles, Materialism, and Poetic Obscurity', *Critical Inquiry* 28 (1): 72–98.

Todorov, Tzvetan (1990) *Genres in Discourse*, trans. Catherine Porter, Cambridge: Cambridge University Press.

Tucker, Herbert (1985) 'Dramatic Monologue and the Overhearing of Lyric', in Hosek and Parker (eds), *op. cit.*, 226–43.

—— (ed.) (1999) *A Companion to Victorian Literature and Culture*, Oxford: Blackwell.

Walker, Jeffrey (1989) 'Aristotle's Lyric: Re-Imagining the Rhetoric of Epideictic Song', *College English* 51 (1): 5–28.

Waller, Gary (1993) *English Poetry of the Sixteenth Century*, 2nd edn, London: Longman.

Watts, Carol (2000) 'Beyond Interpellation? Affect, Embodiment and the Poetics of Denise Riley', in Mark and Rees-Jones (eds), *op. cit.*, 157–72.

Wellek, René (1970) *Discriminations*, New Haven, CT, USA: Yale University Press.

Welsh, Andrew (1978) *Roots of Lyric: Primitive Poetry and Modern Poetics*, Princeton, NJ, USA: Princeton University Press.

Whitmore, Charles E. (1918) 'A Definition of the Lyric', *PMLA* 33 (4): 584–600.

Williams, William Carlos (1967) *Autobiography*, New York: New Directions.

Wilson, Emily (2004) 'Tongue Breaks', *London Review of Books*, 8 January: 27–28.

Wimsatt, W. K. (1970) *The Verbal Icon: Studies in the Meaning of Poetry*, London: Methuen.

Wimsatt, W. K. and Cleanth Brooks (1970) *Literary Criticism: A Short History*, London: Routledge.

Winters, Yvor (1957) *The Function of Criticism: Problems and Exercises*, Denver: Swallow.

Wu, Duncan (ed.) (1998) *A Companion to Romanticism*, Oxford: Blackwell.

Index